MW00627948

The Critical Race Theory $cam

Dissecting a Racist Ideology

Christopher Arend

Disclaimer: All links to sources listed in the footnotes or elsewhere in this book could be accessed as cited at the time the citation was written. However, those cited links may no longer function.

Dedication

For my Parents

Anne L. Arend and Philip H. Arend

I am forever grateful to you for teaching me to despise
racism and value the individual.

Acknowledgment

Thank you to everyone who has provided encouragement
and comments and otherwise helped in this project,
especially Aaron Cantrell and Mark Nelson.

About the Author

Christopher Arend's mother immigrated to the United States from Lwow, Poland (now Lviv, Ukraine) just before World War II, but her parents and brother became victims of the Holocaust. This tragedy was a prime reason for Christopher's father, who served in the Pacific Theater in World War II, and his mother to raise Christopher and his sister to abhor racism and prejudice as they grew up in Northern California in the 1950s and 1960s.

After graduation from Novato High School, California, (class of 1969) and attending junior college at College of Marin for three semesters, Christopher enlisted in the US Army where he was trained as a German translator/interpreter and as an MP (Military Police). He served a total of three years and received an honorable discharge as a sergeant.

Christopher Arend is one of a handful of Americans who ever studied law in both Germany (Johannes-Gutenberg Universität, Mainz, class of 1979) and the United States of America (UC Berkeley Law School, class of 1981). He became fully qualified as a lawyer in both countries and practiced law in a broad range of areas (e.g. corporate, finance, arbitration, IT) in the Frankfurt am Main, Germany, office of a major international law firm. Christopher returned with his wife and son to California at the end of 2004. He has worked primarily as a legal translator since then.

Christopher was elected to the Board of Trustees of the Paso Robles Joint Unified School District where he served from 2018 until 2022. Christopher fought against Critical Race Theory as a school board member and wrote the resolution adopted in August 2021 with which the Paso Robles school board, as perhaps the first local school board in the nation, banned the teaching of Critical Race Theory. Christopher has given many lectures about Critical Race Theory and has written this book as a further contribution to the movement against the racist Critical Race Theory ideology.

CONTACT INFORMATION:

Christopher Arend has set up a blog for this book at:

http://www.stop-scams.us/

You can email Christopher Arend at:

christopher.arend@stop-scams.us

Contents

Introduction

Immediately after the death of George Floyd in May 2020, politicians and the mainstream media started blaming **"systemic racism**." For a large part of the population, the George Floyd death was just another in a series of injustices perpetrated upon "people of color" by an inherently racist system. The only cure to "systemic racism" for many was to destroy the "system."[1] This demand was underscored by a summer of riots and civil unrest throughout the country, ranging from the destruction of large sections of Minneapolis and other major cities to blocking freeways in small towns such as San Luis Obispo, California. In some cities, namely, Seattle and Portland, the local and state governments abdicated their authority to mobs. The violence on the streets was accompanied by a rise in the popularity of books such as *White Fragility* by Robin DiAngelo (2018), *How to be an Antiracist* by Ibram X. Kendi (2019), and *Me and White Supremacy* by Layla F. Saad (2020).

Students across the country started returning to class in the 2020/21 school year with distance learning. For the first time, their parents were able to see directly what their children were being taught. Many parents were shocked at the level of leftist politicization, especially in social studies and English courses. The reaction was swift. Parents across the country, from Fairfax and Louden counties in Virginia to my own town of Paso Robles, California, where a couple of teachers saw fit to display Black Lives Matter banners in their video backgrounds on the first day of school, started voicing strong opposition to the indoctrination of their children. By the early part of 2021, the public discussion moved away from "systemic racism" and zeroed in on **Critical Race Theory** ("CRT"). Conservative state legislatures started passing statutes to ban the teaching of CRT in grades K-12. The resistance against CRT in these grades also took place in local school districts, including in Paso Robles, where I reside.[2]

I was elected to the school board of the Paso Robles Joint Unified School District in 2018 and served until December 2022, including as president of the board in the last two years of my term. Paso Robles Joint Unified School District is located in a well-known wine-growing region on the Central Coast of California, approximately halfway between San Francisco and Los Angeles. In April 2021, our school board adopted a resolution I authored that condemns racism. We also approved at the same time an Ethnic Studies course, which I strongly supported.

At the suggestion of a fellow board member, I subsequently authored a resolution to ban CRT in our schools. I had already been studying the subject for quite some time. The school board adopted the resolution banning CRT on 10 August 2021 after more than two hours of public comment over the course of three separate board meetings. We may have been the first local school board in the country to ban CRT. Fox News reported the story in their national news on 11 August 2021.[3] Traditional mainstream media ignored the story.

Members of the public at the meetings of our school board were passionate in their support of CRT, just as other members of the public were passionate in support of the ban. Although a couple of speakers had read some articles about CRT and had a fair command of superficial talking points, it soon became apparent that the one common aspect on both sides of the issue was that all speakers knew virtually nothing about the actual substance of Critical Race Theory. I was struck by the absurdity of people getting worked up on both sides of the debate without really knowing what they were talking about. This is perhaps an inherent consequence of a smaller national attention span due to the media trading in 30-second soundbites and the pre-Elon Musk Twitter culture.

Critical Race Theory has also benefited from a lack of intellectual challenge in America's universities and colleges. Very few professors have dared to question CRT in their writings, quite possibly due to fear of retaliation. Critical Race Theory, however, is by far the most important ideological debate of our time and threatens to destroy the very foundations of American society.

Critical Race Theory has spread throughout the American system of higher education and is finding its way into grades K-12 under the guise of "DEI" (diversity, equity, inclusion) and "SEL" (social emotional learning). The assault on American history and culture, such as the "1619 Project" and the removal of the statue of Thomas Jefferson from New York's city hall, are direct consequences of CRT. Critical Race Theory has also spurred the growth of the "diversity industry" with countless "diversity consultants" selling high-priced absolution for perceived past sins to corporations and governmental agencies. Critical Race Theory has become the foundation for a shakedown racket that permeates all of American society. More than 100 years ago, Booker T. Washington clearly recognized the way race can be exploited for personal financial gain and social status:

> I am afraid that there is a certain class of race-problem solvers who don't want the patient to get well because as long as the disease holds out, they have not only an easy means of making a living but also an easy medium through which to make themselves prominent before the public.[4]

This book describes the philosophical roots and the substance of Critical Race Theory. However, this book is not intended to be a comprehensive discussion of the various permutations Critical Theory and its predecessors (e.g. the material determinism of Karl Marx) have gone through on the way to becoming Critical Race Theory. James Lindsay's recent book *Race Marxism* provides an excellent, in-depth discussion of the roots of Critical Race Theory in Marxism and the exhaustive debate over the course of at least the last 100 years in academia and among philosophers about Marxism, Critical Theory, and Critical Race Theory.[5]

The fundamental intellectual failings of Critical Race Theory become readily apparent when we look past the smoke and mirrors of the supposedly sophisticated blather used by Marxist philosophers. Critical Theory and, with it, Critical Race Theory are then revealed to be an intellectually vacuous tool for sowing racial animosity while at the same time feeding a multi-billion dollar CRT industry. The own words of the proponents of Critical Race Theory unmask CRT as a truly racist ideology that judges people according to the color of their skin rather than the content of their character. CRT should be consigned to the trash pile of failed ideologies, along with its close totalitarian relatives, communism, and fascism.

---

[1]   "We won't stop until we dismantle the whole racist system", American Friends Service Committee, June 4, 2020, at https://afsc.org/newsroom/we-wont-stop-until-we-dismantle-whole-racist-system.

[2]   UCLA Law School tracks efforts against CRT in a tool "CRT Forward – Tracking the Attack on Critical Race Theory" at https://crtforward.law.ucla.edu/wp-content/uploads/2023/04/UCLA-Law_CRT-Report_Final.pdf.

[3]   Michael Ruiz, "California school board bans critical race theory", Foxnews.com, August 11, 2021, at https://www.foxnews.com/us/california-paso-robles-bans-critical-race-theory.

[4]   Booker T. Washington, *My Larger Education* (1910/11), pp. 119, 120, available at https://docsouth.unc.edu/fpn/washeducation/washing.html#wash102.

---

⁵   James Lindsay, <u>Race Marxism</u>, (2022), published by New
Discourses.

Chapter I

Ideology or Methodology
Critical Theory and Critical Thinking

Why does CRT stand for "Critical Race Theory" and not "Critical Race Thinking"? The answer requires knowing what CRT is. The media are a poor source for defining and understanding CRT. They provide little more than a superficial description. The *New York Times* writes, for example:

> Critical race theory is a concept [which] argues that historical patterns of racism are ingrained in law and other modern institutions and that the legacies of slavery, segregation, and Jim Crow still create an uneven playing field for Black people and other people of color. The idea is that racism is not a matter of individual bigotry but is systemic in America.[1]

The authors of the main textbook on Critical Race Theory provide little more substance when they concede that CRT is a "movement":

> The critical race theory (CRT) movement is a collection of activists and scholars engaged in studying and transforming the relationship between race, racism, and power. ... Unlike traditional civil rights discourse ..., critical race theory questions the very foundations of the liberal order, including equality theory, legal reasoning, Enlightenment rationalism, and neutral principles of constitutional law.2
> (Emphasis added)

Other proponents of CRT provide no additional guidance about the fundamental definition of Critical Race Theory. However, it is clear from just these two quotes that CRT is a system of thought with established tenets and the goal of fundamentally changing society. CRT accordingly falls squarely under the definition of "ideology" because CRT is based on specific, immutable assumptions and is directed towards achieving certain socio-economic goals.[3] The key aspect of any ideology is that it is primarily substantive, i.e. it is based on assumptions of fact that cannot be questioned without shaking the very foundation of the ideology.

This is in stark contrast to a "methodology," i.e. "a body of methods, rules, and postulates employed by a discipline: a particular procedure or set of procedures."[4] The scientific method is typical for a methodology. Facts are observed and analyzed, common aspects are identified and developed into a hypothesis which is then tested with additional observations and experiments. The hypothesis may be augmented, revised, or completely discarded, depending on the result of the testing. An essential aspect of the scientific method and, for that matter, any methodology is that the substantive result obtained by applying the methodology can change as new facts are discovered. Even supposedly universal truths, such as "You can't get something from nothing," may change under further inquiry.[5]

The difference between "ideology" and "methodology" is mirrored in the difference between "critical theory" and "critical thinking." Of course, students should learn critical thinking because that skill will serve them well throughout their lives.

> Critical thinking is the intellectually disciplined process of actively and skillfully conceptualizing, applying, analyzing, synthesizing, and/or evaluating information gathered from, or generated by observation, experience, reflection, reasoning, or communication, as a guide to belief and action. In its exemplary form, it is based on universal intellectual values that transcend subject matter divisions:

clarity, accuracy, precision, consistency, relevance, sound evidence, good reasons, depth, breadth, and fairness.[6]

Supporters of CRT frequently argue that CRT supposedly teaches "critical thinking" about society and history.

Critical race theory, true to its name, teaches critical thinking. Everyone says they want students "to learn how to think." And they should think critically about every area of their lives. Thus, CRT prepares students to recognize the academic and social issues operating in a real-world context. Critical thinking is one of the most important skills employers are looking for today.[7]

This is false because there are fundamental differences between "critical thinking" and "critical theory", although both concepts use the word "critical".

"Critical thinking" is inherently procedural. Critical thinking is a methodology that relies on generally recognized rules of logic, precision in the use of terminology, and evidence. Critical thinking involves revisiting and reexamining conclusions and a willingness to "kick the tires" on intellectual concepts, especially when new facts come to light. Critical thinking requires an inquisitive mind willing to question assumptions and dogma.

"Critical Theory" is inherently substantive. Critical Theory is based on factual assumptions about society and social goals, which cannot be questioned without questioning the validity of Critical Theory itself. The assumptions and goals form the basis of specific teachings about society, which, in turn, form the basis for various proposed policies to achieve the goals.

The distinction between procedure and substance is common in the law. For example, the California Civil Code, as substantive law, determines what constitutes a contract and what the parties to a contract are required to do. The Civil Code does not determine the procedure used in the courts to determine whether a contract exists and what the obligations of the parties are under the contract. The decision-making process, i.e. the methodology used to determine whether specific facts of a case have resulted in a contract, is governed by the California Code of Civil Procedure. The same distinction exists in criminal law. For example, Part 1 of the California Penal Code defines what constitutes a crime, while Part 2 of the Penal Code establishes the procedure used to determine the facts in a specific case and whether the defendant is guilty of a crime.

Philosophical roots of Critical Race Theory – Hegelian and Marxist dialectic

Critical Race Theory is based on philosophical concepts developed especially by the German Philosopher Georg Wilhelm Friedrich Hegel (1770 – 1831) in his mid-thirties, the so-called Hegelian dialectic. Hegel, like most philosophers then and now, wrote German in a style that was hardly understandable in German, a problem that has carried over in the English translations of his work. The 19th-century philosopher Schopenhauer wrote about Hegel's philosophy:

> Now if for this purpose I were to say that the so-called philosophy of this fellow Hegel is a colossal piece of mystification, which will yet provide posterity with an inexhaustible theme for laughter at our times, that it is a pseudo-philosophy paralyzing all mental powers, stifling all real thinking, and, by the most outrageous misuse of language, putting in its place the hollowest, most senseless, thoughtless,

and, as is confirmed by its success, most stupefying verbiage, I should be quite right.[8]

Stated more succinctly: Schopenhauer considers Hegel's philosophy to be a bunch of garbage. Even Hegel apparently agreed with this assessment on his deathbed when he reportedly stated, "There was only one person who ever understood me, and even he didn't understand me."[9] Fortunately, there is no need for a deep dive into Hegel's philosophy to understand how it relates to CRT.

The word "dialectic" uses the prefix "di" which means two or twice. Hegel believed that truth could be determined by analyzing two sides of an issue and identifying and resolving apparent contradictions. This process is similar to overlapping sets in mathematics. Everyone certainly remembers these types of diagrams from school: The two circles are usually described in Hegelian philosophy as "thesis" and "antithesis," and the overlap area is called "synthesis."

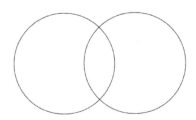

Hegelian dialectic is derived from classical dialectic methods going back to the ancient Greek philosophers such as Plato, Socrates, and Aristotle, but with a subtle yet important difference. The ancient Greek philosophers believed that truth could be revealed in dialogue between proponents of each side of an issue. Classic dialectic is, thus, a methodology. Classic dialectic is readily apparent, for example, in litigation, where each side presents its version of the facts, and the court applies procedural law, such as the rules of evidence, to determine the facts. Hegel applied the fundamental duality of dialectic procedure not as a methodology and instead argued in favor of a substantive dialectic:

> Whereas Plato's "opposing sides" were people (Socrates and his interlocutors), however, what the "opposing sides" are in Hegel's work depends on the **subject matter** he discusses.[10]
> (Emphasis added)

Another German-born philosopher Karl Marx (1818 – 1883), applied Hegelian dialectics to economics and society. Friedrich Engels (1820 – 1895) continued the process and developed the doctrine that came to be known as "dialectic materialism." Marx and Engels observed Western society going through the industrial revolution and divided society into two groups on the basis of substantive criteria, i.e. along a socio-economic dividing line. Marx and Engels considered the "bourgeoisie" to be a relatively small group of people who owned the means of production, while the "proletariat" was the working class and included virtually everyone else in society. Marx and Engels were convinced that the tension between these two classes ("class struggle") would result in the overthrow of the capitalist system. In 1848, when Karl Marx was 30 years old, and Friedrich Engels was 28, they published their *Communist Manifesto* (*Manifest der Kommunistischen Partei*), in which they predicted that the proletariat would overthrow the bourgeoisie and actively called for the violent overthrow of the capitalist system.

This prediction by Marx and Engels did not come true. Capitalism is still the predominant economic system in the world. Furthermore, the first "communist" revolution took place in Russia, which was still a feudal society in the early part of the 20th century. This fundamental failure of Marxist dialectic materialism should have been more than enough reason to discard the doctrine. Critical thinking would have led philosophers, economists, politicians, and society, in general, to recognize that the dialectic materialism of Marx and Engels was simply wrong. There were, however, especially many philosophers in Germany after World War I who could not let go of the dream of watching capitalism collapse. These philosophers came to be known as the "Frankfurt School."

The Frankfurt School and "Critical Theory"

World War I broke out in August of 1914 after the assassination of Archduke Ferdinand of Austria in Sarajevo, at that time a city in the Austro-Hungarian Empire and now part of Bosnia and Herzegovina. The suffering, as well as the economic and social disruption caused by World War I, shattered pre-war social structures throughout Europe. Turmoil in Germany led to the German Revolution of 1918-1919, which swept the Kaiser from power and resulted in the creation of the Weimar Republic. The post-World War I upheaval was especially great in Russia, where the Russian Revolution started in 1917 and culminated in 1922 in the creation of the Union of Soviet Socialist Republics (USSR) under the leadership of Vladimir Lenin and the Communist Party. Lenin consolidated power in the USSR with the brutal suppression of all opposition, while the power structures in the Weimar Republic in Germany devolved into a permanent state of chaos that lasted for more than ten years.

The Frankfurt School was a group of philosophers and social scientists, and other intellectuals who formed the Institute for Social Research (*Institut für Sozialforschung*, the "IfS") under the auspices of the University of Frankfurt am Main in 1923. The building that housed the IfS was originally financed by Felix Weil, using some of the inheritance from his mother's side of the family, while his father financed the personnel. The first director was Carl Grünberg, an internationally recognized Austrian Marxist. The scholars at this institute included Max Horkheimer (1885-1973), Theodor Adorno (1903-1969), Herbert Marcuse (1898-1979), and Erich Fromm (1900-1980), among many others. The IfS was intended to provide an institutional framework for the study of the theory and history of socialism and the workers' movement. The German philosopher Max Horkheimer became the director of the IfS in 1930 and expanded the institute's research from a focus on economics as the foundation of society to covering all aspects of society in an interdisciplinary approach.[11]

German politics soon put an end to the work of the IfS when Adolph Hitler was appointed Chancellor (*Reichskanzler*) on 30 January 1933. Less than six weeks later, on 13 March 1933, the IfS was closed, and its staff members sought refuge in other countries. The institute moved its main offices to Columbia University in 1934, while the members of the IfS continued their work under the leadership of Horkheimer in various countries, including Switzerland, the USA, and England. The IfS returned to Frankfurt shortly after the end of World War II.

Horkheimer developed the term "Critical Theory" in his 1937 essay "Traditional and Critical Theory."[12] He drew a clear distinction between social theories and scientific theories, on the one hand, and "Critical Theory," on the other hand. Horkheimer and critical theorists, in general, argue that social and scientific theories, with their underlying methodology of observation of facts to develop a hypothesis and subsequent empirical verification or falsification of the hypothesis, i.e. the scientific method, create a myth of objectivity about the world and human society because the perception of facts is predetermined by society and the history of the person perceiving the facts.[13] Critical Theory accordingly rejects the concept of objective knowledge and instead views "theory" as subjective.

After trashing the concept that "theory" can embody objective truth, Horkheimer turned to the word "critical." In a typical academic manner, he placed the most fundamental definition of his work, namely, the definition of the term "critical" in a footnote:

> This [human] behavior is referred to hereinafter as "critical." The word is used here less in the sense of idealistic criticism of pure reason and is rather understood in the sense of dialectic criticism of the economy. This word designates an essential aspect of the **dialectic theory** of society.[14]
> (Emphasis added)

Critical Theory developed not just as an approach to understanding society in the past and the present. Critical Theory also claimed responsibility for designing future society for the purpose of supposedly emancipating humanity.[15] The fact that Critical Theory seeks to form society along specific lines means that Critical Theory is intended to evolve into not just a philosophical but also a socio-political "movement" founded on Hegelian and Marxist dialectic.

The fatal flaw in "Critical Theory"

The dialectic approach is both the foundation of Critical Theory as well as the reason why Critical Theory, be it the dialectic materialism of Karl Marx or Critical Race Theory, is a simplistic, intellectually vacuous way of looking at society. The more complex a society, the more a binary dialectic analysis fails to reflect the reality in society and instead becomes a tool for unscrupulous politicians and activists to manipulate base emotions of hate and envy for their own personal gain.

Dialectics first creates two sides constituting "thesis" and "antithesis" in an effort to explain societal phenomena as a "synthesis" resulting from the conflict between two groups. The dialectic of Critical Theory requires dividing society into two groups, namely, the oppressors and the oppressed. Karl Marx used economic wealth as the delineating factor to assign people to either the bourgeoisie as the oppressor class or the proletariat as the oppressed. The proponents of Critical Race Theory use race to divide society into "Whites" and "BIPOC" (Black, Indigenous, and People of Color).

The fundamental intellectual flaw in the dialectic approach to analyzing society is readily apparent without having to delve into the critique of Hegelian dialectics expressed in philosophical writings.[16] The United States of America is a complex society with a population of approximately 330 million people with ethnic origins from throughout the world, living in urban, suburban, and rural communities. Americans have great individual freedom in a country with a high degree of geographic and social mobility and very advanced technology. Splitting American society into two classes along economic lines, like Marx, or along racial lines, like in CRT, completely ignores the complexity of modern American society.

Dialectic is popular with many social scientists in American academia, perhaps because it provides a simplistic framework for their work. Reducing the complexity of American society to only two camps, the oppressed and the oppressors, and relating them to each other, just like comparing two sets of overlapping data in a high school math course, is much easier than searching for overlaps among 330 million sets of data, namely, individual Americans.

Dialectics has also failed as a means of accurately analyzing society. The dialectic materialism of Karl Marx completely failed when it predicted the communist revolution would take place in Western industrialized society. Instead of revisiting the fundamental question of whether dialectics is an appropriate tool for analyzing society, the Marxist ideologues in the Frankfurt School and their progeny decided that dividing society into oppressors and oppressed on the basis of economic class needed to be replaced by finding another criterion for assigning people to the oppressor class or the oppressed class. Race has now become the determinative criterion.

Human society, in general, and especially American society, is far too complex to be analyzed by using one factor to put 330 million people in just two classes. Instead, the complexity of our society is much better reflected by the definition of "chaos theory," known in popular culture for the "butterfly effect."[17]

> Chaos theory is one of the fundamental theories in our lives. It is the study of complex, nonlinear dynamic systems. It is a branch of mathematics that deals with systems that appear to be orderly (deterministic) but, in fact, harbor chaotic behaviors. It also deals with systems that appear to be chaotic but, in fact, have an underlying order.[18]

Chaos theory has, in fact, found its way into the social sciences, especially as a means for solving the inadequacies of more simple models in the field.[19] However, American academia, at least in the social sciences, still seems to favor Critical Theory, now in the guise of Critical Race Theory, with its simplistic approach and emotionally laden rhetoric, over engaging in the intellectually much more strenuous effort required for applying chaos theory and other complex methods of "critical thinking" when analyzing American society. The necessary consequence is a fundamentally simpleminded, inaccurate view of modern American society and an inability to accurately identify the causes of social problems and how to solve them.

Dialectic analysis involves dividing society into two groups, the oppressors and the oppressed, or "us" and "them" and is, therefore, inherently divisive. The dialectic approach does not tolerate people outside the two classes, i.e. people who are neither oppressors nor oppressed. As one of the leading CRT proponents, Ibram X. Kendi writes for our time:

> [T]here is no neutrality in the racism struggle. The opposite of "racist" isn't "not racist." It's "antiracist." What's the difference? One endorses either the idea of a racial hierarchy as a racist or racial equality as an antiracist. One either believes problems are rooted in groups of people, as a racist or locates the roots of problems in power and policies, as an antiracist. One either allows racial inequities to persevere as a racist or confronts racial inequities as an antiracist. There is no in-between safe space of "not racist." The claim of "not racist" neutrality is a mask for racism.[20]

This is the language of an ideological political movement demanding allegiance, not the language of a methodology for applying critical thinking to the analysis of history and society. Dialectics necessarily means, "You're either with us or against us." Despots have used this approach from the dawn of time to garner support, eliminate internal opposition, and gain power. Charlatans have profited since the dawn of time from selling supposed moral redemption to adherents of their ideology and threatening opponents with damnation. Critical Race Theory, as an ideology based on dialectics, is just another in a long line of scams.

Chapter Summary

The reason that "CRT" stands for Critical Race Theory and not "Critical Race Thinking" is that "critical thinking" and "critical theory" are completely different. Critical thinking is a **methodology** based on rational, evidence-based analysis. Critical Race Theory is an **ideology** with certain assumptions written in stone and the basis for a political movement. Critical Race Theory represents a fundamentally simplistic, dialectic view that divides society into "oppressors" and "oppressed." Karl Marx and later his acolytes in the Frankfurt School in post-World War I Germany constituted the ideological nursery in which Critical Race Theory was born. They divided society along an economic line into the bourgeoisie and the proletariat. Critical Race Theory divides society along a racial line into "Whites" and BIPOC.

---

[1]   Lauren Jackson, "What is critical race theory", *The New York Times – The Daily Newsletter*, July 9, 2021, updated on August 18, 2021, https://www.nytimes.com/2021/07/09/podcasts/the-daily-newsletter-critical-race-theory.html.

[2]   Richard Delgado and Jean Stefancic, **Critical Race Theory – An introduction**, 3rd ed. (2017), New York University Press, pg. 3 (cited below as "Delgado/Stefancic").

[3]   See, for a detail discussion of the term "ideology": Cranston, Maurice. "ideology". Encyclopedia Britannica, 27 Oct. 2020, https://www.britannica.com/topic/ideology-society, accessed on December 6, 2021.

[4]   Definition no. 1 in Merriam-Webster at https://www.merriam-webster.com/dictionary/methodology

[5]   See, e.g., Lawrence Krauss, A Universe from Nothing, Free Press (2012).

[6]   "Defining Critical Thinking" at The Foundation for Critical Thinking, citing the National Council for Excellence in Critical

Thinking and a statement by Michael Scriven and Richard Paul at the 8th Annual International Conference on Critical Thinking and Education Reform (1987), https://www.criticalthinking.org/pages/defining-critical-thinking/766.

[7]   Ebony McGee, Devin White, Lynette Parker, "We Taught Critical Race Theory", Inside Higher Ed, September 28, 2021 at https://www.insidehighered.com/views/2021/09/28/what-white-students-say-about-critical-race-theory-course-opinion.

[8]   Arthur Schopenhauer, *On the Basis of Morality*, trans. E.F.J. Payne, Hackett Publishing (1998) pg.15, https://books.google.com/books?id=ye8wNs2kELYC&printsec=frontc over&source=gbs_ge_summary_r&cad=0#v=onepage&q&f=false.

[9]   "Nur ein Mensch hat mich je verstanden. Und auch der verstand mich nicht." (quoted in Der Spiegel 1/1963 at https://www.spiegel.de/kultur/am-jenseits-a-ad33ed62-0002-0001-0000-000045142029.

[10]   Julie Maybee, "Hegel's Dialectics", Stanford Encyclopedia of Philosophy, first published June 3, 2016, substantive revision Oct. 3, 2020, https://plato.stanford.edu/entries/hegel-dialectics/.

[11]   The history of the IfS is available at http://www.ifs.uni-frankfurt.de/institut/geschichte/ (the website is currently (>May 2023) "under construction".

[12]   Max Horkheimer, "Traditionelle und kritische Theorie" (1937), available as a pdf document at http://lesekreis.blogsport.de/images/MaxHorkheimerTraditionelleundkr itischeTheorie.pdf.

[13]   Ibid., pg. 13 "*Die Tatsachen, welche die Sinne uns zuführen, sind in doppelter Weise gesellschaftlich präformiert: durch den geschichtlichen Charakter des wahrgenommenen Gegenstands und den geschichtlichen Charakter des wahrnehmenden Organs.*" (The facts which our senses present to us are pre-formed by society in two ways: by the historical nature of the perceived object and by the historical nature of the perceiving organ. – own translation).

[14]   Ibid., there in footnote 1 on pg. 19 "*Dieses Verhalten wird im folgenden als das »kritische« bezeichnet. Das Wort wird hier weniger im Sinn der idealistischen Kritik der reinen Vernunft als in dem der dialektischen Kritik der Ökonomie verstanden. Es bezeichnet eine wesentliche Eigenschaft der dialektischen Theorie der Gesellschaft.*" (own translation).

[15]   Herbert Marcuse, "Philosophy and Critical Theory" (*Philosphie und Kritische Theorie*), 1937, in *Zeitschrift für*

Sozialforschung, vol. VI, pg. 644, "Das Interesse der kritischen Theorie an der Befreiung der Menschheit ..." (The interest of critical theory in the emancipatiion of humanity ... – own translation); "Die kritische Theorie hat es in bisher nicht gekanntem Masse mit der Vergangenheit zu tun, - gerade sofern es ihr um die Zukunft geht." (Critical theory deals with the past in a degree not previously known – specifically to the extent that critical theory is concerned about the future. – own translation),
https://archive.org/details/ZeitschriftFrSozialforschung6.Jg/page/n685/mode/2up.

[16]   For example, Karl Popper, *The Open Society and its Enemies - Vol. 2 – The High tide of Prophecy: Hegel, Marx, and the Aftermath* (1st ed. 1944) chapter 12 "Hegel and the new tribalism" (pp. 25 et seq.) https://antilogicalism.com/wp-content/uploads/2018/04/open-society-2.pdf (now in the 5th rev. ed., 1966); Mario Augusto Bunge, *"A Critique of Dialectics"* in *Scientific Materialism, D. Reidel Publishing (1981) pp. 41-63,*
https://archive.org/details/scientificmateri0000bung/mode/2up.

[17]   This term is generally considered to have its origin in the Ray Bradbury short story *A Sound of Thunder* in Colliers magazine, June 28, 1952, and has now become well-known due to the 2004 movie *The Butterfly Effect*.

[18]   Hena Rani Biswas, Md. Maruf Hasan, Shujit Kumar Bala, "Chaos, Theory and its Applications in our Real Life", Barishal University Journal Part 1, 5 (1&2): 123-140 (2018) at pp. 123, 124,
https://bu.ac.bd/uploads/BUJ1V5I12/6.%20Hena%20Rani%20Biswas.pdf.

[19]   Ashley Crossman, Ashley. "Chaos Theory." ThoughtCo, April 16, 2019, https://www.thoughtco.com/chaos-theory-3026621#:~:text=In%20the%20social%20sciences%2C%20chaos,linear%20systems%20of%20social%20complexity.&text=Chaos%20theory%20looks%20at%20this,are%20similar%20to%20each%20other.

[20]   Ibram X. Kendi, How to be an Antiracist, Random House (2019), pp. 14, 15.

Chapter II

The Birth of Critical Race Theory

"Critical Theory" comes to America

The quarter century from the end of World War II to 1970 saw a tremendous upheaval in Western society, in general, and especially in the United States. The changes in the area of civil rights in America were nothing short of revolutionary. World War II had shown that America desperately needed the efforts and contributions of all Americans to defeat mortal enemies. African Americans have fought in all of America's wars since the American Revolution. George Washington recognized the need for more manpower and lifted a restriction on African-Americans serving in the Continental Army in January 1776, even before the Declaration of Independence was written.[1] The British also recognized the importance of African-American support. They issued edicts promising freedom to any slaves joining the British cause. Historians estimate that approximately 20,000 African Americans joined the British forces while approximately 5,000 fought with the Continental Army.[2] African-Americans fought in all subsequent wars of the United States, albeit mostly in segregated units until after World War II.

World War II pushed the demand for America's economic and human resources to a level that had not been seen since the Civil War. The United States had a population of just over 132 million when World War II started.[3] A total of approximately 16 million Americans served as members of the military during World War II, and almost 10% of the US population (12,209,238) was in the military in 1945.[4] More than 900,000 African Americans served in the military during this period, mostly in segregated units such as the Tuskegee Airmen and the 92nd and 93rd infantry divisions.[5] It became clear to the nation's leaders, after demilitarization following the end of World War II and the new challenges for the US military at the start of the Cold War, that segregation had no place in the US military. President Truman issued Executive Order 9981 on 26 July 1948, which forbade racial discrimination in the US military, including all related civilian functions such as military schools.[6]

Civilian society in America was not far behind the US military. Race relations in the United States had been based on the doctrine of "separate but equal" which had become firmly established in American constitutional law after the 1896 decision of the Supreme Court in *Plessy v. Ferguson* (163 U.S. 537). [7] The Supreme Court held in that case that, although the 14th Amendment had prohibited racial discrimination by governmental agencies, separate accommodations supposedly did not constitute discrimination so long as the separate accommodations were equal. This "separate but equal" doctrine came under increased opposition in postwar America, and by the early 1950s, litigation had been commenced in several states challenging the constitutionality of "separate but equal" education. The cases from Delaware, Kansas, Virginia, and South Carolina were combined before the US Supreme Court, which unanimously ruled in 1954 in the case *Brown v. Board of Education of Topeka* (347 U.S. 483) that the "separate but equal" doctrine did not apply in the field of education and that segregated schools were inherently unequal.[8]

The *Brown v. Board of Education* decision was limited only to segregation in public schools and did not universally eliminate the concept of "separate but equal." However, this unanimous Supreme Court decision paved the way for other efforts to eliminate racial discrimination throughout American society. One year later, on December 1, 1955, a 42-year-old seamstress and member of the National

Association for the Advancement of Colored People (NAACP) in Montgomery, Alabama, Ms. Rosa Parks, challenged "separate but equal" when she famously refused to give up her seat in the black section of a bus to a white man because the seats in the white section at the front of the bus were full. Her arrest and the subsequent boycott of the privately owned local bus system by the African-American population of Montgomery led to the founding of the Montgomery Improvement Association, which elected a newly arrived pastor Dr. Martin Luther King Jr. to lead the organization. The Montgomery bus system was integrated on December 20, 1955, after the Supreme Court, in *Browder v. Gayle*, 352 U.S. 903 (1955), summarily dismissed an appeal against the decision of the Federal District Court, which had ruled that segregation in the Montgomery bus system violated the 14th Amendment.

> We hold that the statutes and ordinances requiring segregation of the white and colored races on the motor buses of a common carrier of passengers in the City of Montgomery and its police jurisdiction violate the due process and equal protection of the law clauses of the Fourteenth Amendment to the Constitution of the United States. [9]

Rosa Parks became known as the "First Lady of civil rights" and the "Mother of the freedom movement" and was eventually awarded the Congressional Gold Medal in 1999.[10]

Dr. Martin Luther King Jr. became the leader of the civil rights movement, driving the push to eliminate racial segregation under the "separate but equal" doctrine in all aspects of American life. He gave his "I Have a Dream" speech in Washington, D.C., in 1963 and, perhaps more eloquently than anyone else in American history, expressed the fundamental promise of equality before the law embodied in the 14th Amendment to the U.S. Constitution:

> I have a dream that my four little children will one day live in a nation where they will not be judged by the color of their skin but by the content of their character.[11]

The landmark Civil Rights Act of 1964, following initial civil rights legislation previously passed, such as the Civil Rights Acts of 1957 and 1960, effectively put an end to racial discrimination in American law. The Civil Rights Act of 1968, commonly referred to as the Fair Housing Act, prohibited racial discrimination in housing. Legislation in the individual states and litigation before federal and state courts eliminated race discrimination in the law and, to a great extent, in actual practice by the early 1970s. Fifty years and two generations later, it is impossible to find laws and regulations now in effect that discriminate on the basis of race, except for the occasional attempts in some public agencies to give preferential treatment to ethnic minorities (affirmative action).

Not all Americans agreed with the efforts of the civil rights movement. Aside from the typical and often violent resistance by white racists in the Ku Klux Klan and other organizations, predominantly in the states that had once constituted the Confederate States of America in the Civil War, there was also a strong black separatist and nationalist movement that considered the elimination of racial segregation and prejudice to be an illusory goal and instead supported physical or at least cultural separation of the races. The Nation of Islam and the Black Panther Party believed that only separation from the rest of the American population would yield salvation for African-Americans.[12]

The 1960s and the first few years of the 1970s saw not only great changes in the field of civil rights. American culture, in general, and especially America's universities, were experiencing change to an extent and rapidity never before seen. The movement against the Vietnam War merged with the civil rights movement, while cheering at the same time for black separatists. The widespread disdain for communism in the early phases of the Cold War had given way to tolerance and even open support of Marxism. The iconic images of Black Panthers leader Huey Newton and the Marxist revolutionary Che Guevara were proudly displayed on college campuses throughout the country.

Che Guevara   Huey Newton

American academia was fertile ground for the spread of Critical Theory. Herbert Marcuse and other representatives of the Frankfurt School were welcomed with open arms in academia. Marcuse worked in the Frankfurt School's Geneva office in 1932 and moved to the branch of the Frankfurt School at Columbia University in 1933. He worked for the Office of Strategic Services during World War II as an analyst focusing on Nazi Germany and subsequently worked at the U.S. Department of State. Marcuse returned to academia in 1952 with teaching assignments as a political analyst at leading universities such as Columbia, Harvard, and then Brandeis (1954–1965) and finally at the University of California in San Diego. His outspoken nature and his fervent support for revolutionary change made him the idol of the youthful intellectual left ("We have to develop the political implications of the moral, intellectual, and sexual rebellion of the youth.")[13]

Critical Theory spread throughout academia, including to law schools. This led directly to the development of "Critical Legal Studies" ("CLS"), sometimes referred to as "Critical Legal Theory" ("CLT"). The fact that CLS is founded on Critical Theory and dialectics is readily apparent from the following two definitions of CLS in online publications of two leading American universities. The dialectic split between oppressed and oppressors is expressly reflected in the first quote by using the words "privileged" and "underprivileged," and the philosophical roots of CLS in Marxism and Critical Theory are expressly mentioned in the second quote.

> Critical legal studies (CLS) is a theory which states that the law is necessarily intertwined with social issues, particularly stating that the law has inherent social biases. Proponents of CLS believe that the law supports the interests of those who create the law. As such, CLS states that the law supports a power dynamic which favors the historically privileged and disadvantages the historically underprivileged. CLS finds that the wealthy and the powerful use the law as an instrument for oppression in order to maintain their place in hierarchy. Many in the CLS movement want to overturn the hierarchical structures of modern society and they focus on the law as a tool in achieving this goal.[14]

Some critical scholars adapt ideas drawn from Marxist and socialist theories to demonstrate how economic power relationships influence legal practices and consciousness. For others, the Frankfurt School of Critical Theory and its attention to the construction of cultural and psycho-social meanings are central to explaining how law uses mechanisms of denial and legitimation.[15]

Derrick Bell, the father of CRT

The most influential person in the development of Critical Race Theory is generally considered to be Derrick Bell (1930–2011). He joined the civil rights division at the United States Department of Justice shortly after graduating from law school in 1957. He was asked in 1959 to resign his membership in the NAACP because of concerns that the membership could be used to argue that the federal authorities were biased in civil rights litigation. Bell instead resigned from the Department of Justice and soon took a position with the NAACP Legal Defense and Education Fund in 1960. He started an academic career at the USC law school in 1967, moving on to Harvard Law School as a lecturer in 1969 and becoming the first tenured African-American professor at Harvard Law School in 1971. Derrick Bell's active career continued until his death in 2011 from cancer at the age of 80. His book *Race and Racism in American Law*, published originally in 1973 and now in its 6th printing, became a foundational work in Critical Race Theory. Derrick Bell is credited with defining one of the core assumptions in CRT, namely, "interest convergence" (discussed below in Chapter IV point 2). The following quote from the Wikipedia entry for Derrick Bell leaves no doubt about the philosophical basis of Critical Race Theory:

Bell and other legal scholars began using the phrase "critical race theory" (CRT) in the 1970s as a takeoff on "critical legal theory," a branch of legal scholarship that challenges the validity of concepts such as rationality, objective truth, and judicial neutrality. Critical legal theory was itself a takeoff on critical theory, a philosophical framework with roots in Marxist thought.[16]

Chapter Summary

American society started to make strides toward integration after World War II. Dr. Martin Luther King, building on the success of *Brown v. Board of Education* and the Civil Rights movement, defeated Jim Crow by the late 1960s. The concept of equal treatment before the law, expressed by Dr. King in his "I Have a Dream" speech in Washington, D.C., in 1963, had finally been achieved in the American legal system. However, there was also a strong black separatist movement represented by organizations such as the Black Panthers and the Nation of Islam. During the same period, Critical Theory, which had come to America with members of the Frankfurt School fleeing the Nazis, was spreading in American universities; Herbert Marcuse was a star by the late 1960s. The divisive dialectic of Critical Theory was a good match for the sentiment embodied in the black separatist movement. Professor Derrick Bell applied Critical Theory as a tool for the purpose of analyzing law and society through the lens of race. His Critical Legal Studies spread initially through law schools and have now expanded throughout academia under the name of Critical Race Theory.

---

[1]   Dr. Greg Bradsher, "African Americans and the American War for Independence" (January 8, 2013) in National Archives – The Text Message, https://text-

message.blogs.archives.gov/2013/01/08/african-americans-and-the-american-war-for-independence/.

2   Christopher Klein, "How Enslaved Men Who Fought for the British Were Promised Freedom" (updated version of September 28, 2021) in History.com, https://www.history.com/news/the-ex-slaves-who-fought-with-the-british.

3   US Census, https://www.census.gov/history/www/through_the_decades/fast_facts/1940_fast_facts.html.

4   The numbers on World War II participation are available at the site of the National World War II Museum at https://www.nationalww2museum.org/students-teachers/student-resources/research-starters/research-starters-us-military-numbers.

5   Ibid.

6   Copy of Executive Order 9881 available at https://en.wikipedia.org/wiki/Executive_Order_9981#/media/File:Executive_Order_9981.jpg.

7   Plessy v. Ferguson, 163 U.S. 537. https://tile.loc.gov/storage-services/service/ll/usrep/usrep163/usrep163537/usrep163537.pdf.

8   "We conclude that, in the field of public education, the doctrine of "separate but equal" has no place. Separate educational facilities are inherently unequal." *Brown v. Board of Education of Topeka*, 347 U.S. *483 (1954), pg. 495, https://supreme.justia.com/cases/federal/us/347/483/.*

9   *Browder v. Gayle*, 142 F. Supp. 707 (M.D. Ala. 1956), https://law.justia.com/cases/federal/district-courts/FSupp/142/707/2263463/.

10   Public Law 106-26 of 4 May 1999, available at https://www.govinfo.gov/content/pkg/PLAW-106publ26/html/PLAW-106publ26.htm.

11   "I have a dream" speech on August 28, 1963 in Washington, D.C., full text at https://www.aol.com/article/news/2017/01/16/dr-martin-luther-kings-i-have-a-dream-speech-full-text/21655947/.

12   See e.g. Claude A. Clegg, III, "Message from the Wilderness of North America: Elijah Muhammed and the nation of Islam, c. 1960" in The Journal for MultiMedia History, vol. 1 no. 1 Fall 1998, with the a transcript of a radio speech by Elijah Muhammed on November 23, 1960 at https://www.albany.edu/jmmh/vol1no1/elijahmuhammad.html.

---

[13]   This statement was made in 1967 during a visit to West Germany. Quoted by Thomas Bourne in "Herbert Marcuse – Grandfather of the New Left", in *Change*, 11:6 (September 1979), pg. 37, https://web.archive.org/web/20200709231432/https://www.marcuse.or g/herbert/booksabout/70s/Bourne1979MarcuseGrandfatherNewLeft.pdf .

[14]   Cornell Law School, Legal Information Institute, https://www.law.cornell.edu/wex/critical_legal_theory.

[15]   Harvard University, The Bridge, available at https://cyber.harvard.edu/bridge/CriticalTheory/critical2.htm.

[16]   Available at https://en.wikipedia.org/wiki/Derrick_Bell#cite_note-7. Citing Wikipedia is often unacceptable in academic research papers due to the open nature of Wikipedia entries, However, Wikipedia is a readily accessible and useful source (see for more information on citing Wikipedia: https://en.wikipedia.org/wiki/Wikipedia:Academic_use).

Chapter III

"Racism" Redefined[1]

The term "systemic racism" became popular in the summer of 2020 after the killing of George Floyd and the ensuing civil unrest. The Democratic Party, the mainstream media, and, of course, the Black Lives Matter movement argue that America was founded on racism and that all society is still permeated by "systemic racism." The proponents of this view go so far as to say that denying the existence of "systemic racism" is itself racist.[2]

Most Americans see no signs of "systemic racism" in our society. They feel no personal, racial prejudice and point to civil rights legislation and court decisions that outlawed racial discrimination in government and the private economy over 50 years ago. Most Americans acknowledge the existence of a few white supremacists in the country, but their number is insignificant and especially rare in our law enforcement agencies. If a law enforcement officer is found to be driven by racial prejudice, that officer is disciplined and usually removed from the force.

These opposing views result from fundamentally different definitions of the basic term "racism." While the general public understands "racism" in the traditional sense of the term, Critical Race Theory and the political left apply a new definition of "racism" developed by the academic world and activist organizations over the last five decades. This new definition is the cornerstone of "systemic racism" and plays an essential role in Critical Race Theory. The new definition, however, is an artificial construct that has no rational basis and leads to absurd results. However, the new definition is the linchpin for the concept of "systemic racism" and broader Critical Race Theory. Both the concept of "systemic racism" as well as CRT are, in essence, nothing more than transparent, intellectual contortions intended to sow division in the United States of America in true dialectic fashion while causing immeasurable harm, specifically to the people who the political left supposedly wants to help.

Traditional definition of "racism":

There are few tasks more tedious than a lengthy discussion about the definition of one word, but understanding the definitions of the common words "racism," "racist" and "race" is essential to understanding the concepts of "systemic racism" and critical race theory.[3] Unless definitions of terms are clearly understood, all further discussion is often a fruitless exercise. That is why lawyers and legislators put a great deal of effort into having exactly "defined terms" in statutes and contracts.

The Webster online dictionary defines **"racism"** as follows:[4]

Noun 1.   racism – the prejudice that members of one race are intrinsically superior to members of other races.

2.   a doctrine or political program based on the assumption of racism and designed to execute its principles

The Webster online dictionary defines **"racist"** as follows:[5]

Noun 1.   Racist - a person with a prejudiced belief that one race is superior to others
Synonyms: racialist

Adj. 1.   Racist - based on racial intolerance; "racist remarks"

2.   racist - discriminatory especially on the basis of race or religion

Synonyms: anti-Semite, anti-black, anti-Semitic

The main element in both definitions is "**race**." Although commonly used in the USA to differentiate between large ethnic groups, e.g. "white," "black," "brown," "Asian" or between "people of color" and everyone else, the term "race" actually has a more abstract meaning when used to refer to a group of people:[6]

 1 a: any one of the groups that humans are often divided into based on physical traits regarded as common among people of shared ancestry

  b: a group of people sharing a common cultural, geographical, linguistic, or religious origin or background

According to this definition, any group of people with any common features that are different from another group can be considered to be a "race." The commonalities do not have to be physical features such as skin tone. Culture, religion, language, country of origin, and any other aspect or combination of aspects can be a sufficient commonality for one group to view another group as constituting a different "race." A "race" can be large and inclusive or very specific, depending on the criteria chosen to delineate "race."

The broad meaning of the term "race" is exemplified in the statement attributed to Rosa Parks, "I believe there is only one race – the human race."[7] This statement implies that different physical features between groups of people should not matter because we are all finally members of the same species. The great civil rights movement in the 1950s and 1960s was built on this principle. Human beings, of course, obviously share common characteristics because all humans are members of the species *homo sapiens*. However, there are also countless subgroups of humans within the species.

Many groups have common physical or cultural characteristics compared to other groups. These groups accordingly have the potential for being designated as separate "races." Common physical features are, in fact, the reason why terms such as "white," brown," "black" and other colors are used to designate different "races" both in the United States as well as throughout the rest of the world.

Recognizing that groups of people exist who share common characteristics and referring to those groups as "races" is no more immoral than recognizing the existence of anything else in the world. The television comedian Stephen Colbert famously made a joke out of the statement in 2014, "I am not a racist. I don't even see race ... not even my own." [8] It is, indeed, impossible for anyone to avoid the conclusion that there are different groups of individuals who share certain physical characteristics. Morality and human decency with regard to "race" are determined by how we treat individuals in various groups and not by the fact that we identify different groups.

Race as a "social construct"

Critical Race Theory defines "race" as a "social construct" with which individuals are classified in society as belonging to a certain group based on one or more common characteristics.

> [T]he "social construction" thesis holds that race and races are products of social thought and relations. Not objective, inherent, or fixed, they correspond to no biological or genetic reality; rather, races are categories that society invents, manipulates, or retires when convenient. [9]

This definition of "race" is generally consistent with the traditional definition, i.e. "a class or kind of people unified by shared ... characteristics." However, Critical Race

Theory conflates the definition of "race" with additional elements derived from the dialectic origins of CRT that serve the ideological purpose of drawing a line between the "oppressor" class and the "oppressed" class. The above-quoted CRT definition implies that society purposefully "invents" races when "convenient." The author Ibram X. Kendi actually rejects the term "social construct" in favor of the term "power construct" when he defines "race" as: "A power construct of collected or merged difference that lives socially."[10]

Adding the concept of "power" to the definition of "race" and especially to the definition of "racism" logically precludes using these terms in any other context where "power" might be completely irrelevant. A further implication of the CRT definitions of "race" and "racism" is that any society with two or more "races" has necessarily allocated power on the basis of "race" and "racism" because "power" is an essential element in the CRT definitions.

Focusing on power ignores the fact that differences in appearance result from different ethnic origins of groups of people in different regions of the world over the course of the evolution of the human species and that these differences in appearance and ethnic origin can, for example, be a relevant factor in genetic epidemiology and the study of certain genetic disorders such as sickle-cell anemia (most common in people with sub-Saharan ancestry), cystic fibrosis (most common among people of Northern European ancestry), Tay-Sachs disease (most common among Ashkenazi Jews and certain other groups) and Finnish heritage diseases.

Merely recognizing that there are various races is not "racism." If that were the case, everyone would have to be considered racist since every person recognizes common characteristics among individuals belonging to different groups of people. The terms "racist" and "racism" would be equivalent to saying that anyone with a command of their senses is automatically a "racist." These highly pejorative terms gain their meaning from the additional element of "prejudice," i.e. "a preconceived judgment or opinion" or "an adverse opinion or leaning formed without just grounds or before sufficient knowledge."[11]

The CRT definition of "racism"

The new definition of racism starts with the elements of "race" and "prejudice" but adds a third element, "power." The new definition was developed in academia in the 1970s and is often reduced to the equation "prejudice + power = racism," whereby the element "prejudice" is understood to mean racial prejudice.

> Contrary to a dictionary definition, racism, as defined based on social science research and theory, is about much more than race-based prejudice—it exists when an imbalance in power and social status is generated by how we understand and act upon race.[12]

> But such an understanding ignores the real factor behind racism (as well as sexism). Power! Racism (and sexism) are not about color or gender; they are about Power![13]

Credit for first postulating that "racism" is more than the traditional definition and consists of (racial) prejudice *plus* power is generally attributed to the 1970 book *Developing New Perspectives on Race* by the academic psychologist Patricia Bidol-Padva,[14]

This begs the question, what is meant by the term "power"? The new definition uses the element "power" to refer to the actual ability of one ethnic group to impose its prejudice on other ethnic groups in society, be it by means of the law or other means.

By power we mean: the authority granted through social structures and conventions—possibly supported by force or the threat of force—and access to means of communications and resources to reinforce racial prejudice, regardless of the falsity of the underlying prejudiced assumption. Basically, all power is relational, and the different relationships either reinforce or disrupt one another.[15]

Power, in its essence, is the capacity to act. Sociologically, power comes in two forms, coercive and choice. In its coercive form, it is the capacity to act in a manner that influences the behavior of others, even against their wishes. This is material power, the most prevalent and destructive form of power in society today, and appeals to the baser qualities of human beings because of competition over scarce resources. Power as choice, on the other hand, is the capacity to act in a manner that influences the behavior of others without violating free moral choice. This is moral power, which appeals to the higher faculties of humankind. This type of power gives rise to true power. "True power is knowing that you can, but you don't." To practice this form of power is the height of self-control. Once one understands that racism at its core has to do with power, one will then recognize that at the root of racism lie two important elements, the material and moral basis of oppression.[16]

The doctrine that "power" must be reflected in the definition of "racism" is now under consideration in the Merriam-Webster dictionary.[17]

> When a racial group's collective prejudice is backed by the power of legal authority and institutional control, it is transformed into racism, a far-reaching system that functions independently from the intentions or self-images of individual actors.[18]

The proponents of the new CRT definition of "racism" necessarily divide society into different races, i.e. ethnic groups, or at least into "Whites" and "people of color" (i.e. everyone who is not "white," often also referred to as "POC" or "BIPOC").[19] It is axiomatic for the proponents of the new definition (consistent with the dialectics of "oppressed" and "oppressors") that the "white" race in the United States is the only race with the "power" to impose prejudices on POC.

> White people in North America live in a society that is deeply separate and unequal by race, and white people are the beneficiaries of that separation and inequality. …Given how seldom we experience racial discomfort **in a society we dominate** … (Emphasis added)[20]

When the proponents of the new definition speak about one race having the power to control society to the exclusion of other races, this generality is attributed to all individuals in that race, with the result that all members of the race are considered to be "racists." This type of general assessment of all people belonging to an ethnic group is, *per se,* an example of racism under the traditional definition, i.e. judging someone by the color of their skin.

> A racist is one who is both privileged and socialized on the basis of race by a white supremacist (racist) system. The term applies to all white people (i.e., people of European descent) living in the United States, regardless of class, gender, religion, culture, or sexuality. By this definition, people of color cannot be racists because, as people within the U.S.

system, they do not have the power to back up their prejudices, hostilities, or acts of discrimination. (This does not deny the existence of such prejudices, hostilities, acts of rage, or discrimination.)[21]

Consequences of the two different definitions of "racism"

"Racist" is one of the most emotionally laden accusations that can be made against a person in today's American society, and indeed throughout western civilization. The First Amendment of the U.S. Constitution generally allows public expression of racist sentiments and protects racist speech from government sanction.[22] Although the law does not punish racist speech in America, our society is quick to fire employees and otherwise punish expressions of racism or even statements and actions that possibly imply a potential racist bent (so-called "cancel culture"). Other countries are more restrictive and impose criminal penalties on racist speech. For example, making anti-Muslim comments has been charged as the crime of making "malicious comments" in Great Britain,[23] and the German Criminal Code (*Strafgesetzbuch*) in § 130 punishes the incitement of hatred against racial groups.[24] In light of the serious consequences for anyone accused of racism, great care should be taken before making such an accusation. The results of the two definitions of "racism" on the analysis of "systemic racism" and government policy accordingly deserve closer scrutiny.

Individual or collective guilt?

Just as it would be unconstitutional to find members of a group collectively guilty of a crime when individual members of the group have nothing to do with the crime, the guilt of being a "racist" should only be ascribed to individuals and not to all members of a large ethnic group.

The difference between individual guilt and collective guilt is one of the major aspects that shows the difference between the two definitions of racism.

The **traditional definition** provides a reasonable basis for accusing an individual of a moral failing when that person expresses racial prejudice. The principle expressed in the Golden Rule is a foundational moral principle: "Do unto others as you would have them do unto you."[25] No individual wishes to be judged on the basis of race rather than on the basis of character. A person who engages in racially prejudiced acts violates this fundamental moral principle. The still current dictionary definition of "racist" as a noun specifically refers to an individual "person." The current dictionary definition of "racism" refers to "a belief." Although one or more individuals can have a racist "belief," attributing a racist belief to someone merely because they are a member of an ethnic group, even though that individual does not share the belief, is irrational. The view that all members of an ethnic group have the same beliefs because they belong to a specific ethnic group is itself "racist" under the traditional definition. The individualist nature of the traditional definition forms the basis of Dr. Martin Luther King's perhaps most quoted statement:

> I have a dream that my four little children will one day live in a nation where they will not be judged by the color of their skin but by the content of their character.[26]

The **new definition** rejects the individualist approach and instead attributes racism collectively to the majority race that supposedly controls the "system." The new definition cannot serve as a basis for an accusation of personal moral fault because virtually no individual alone can satisfy the element of "power" in the new definition. The new definition can only ascribe collective moral failing to the ethnic group that supposedly has the "power." From there, it is only a short step to individualizing the collective guilt and attributing "racism" to every individual in the controlling ethnic group. This is readily apparent in the case of popular authors such as Robin DiAngelo (*White Fragility*) and others who attribute collective guilt merely on the basis of race. She said in an interview on Michigan Radio in 2015, three years before her book *White Fragility* was published in 2018:

> "Racism comes out of our pores as white people. It's the way we are." [27]

This – under the old definition - blatantly racist concept has found its way into academia:

> "The term [racist] applies to all white people (i.e., people of European descent) living in the United States, regardless of class, gender, religion, culture or sexuality."[28]

Racists and racism are stupid.

The element of "prejudice" (i.e. making a judgment or having an opinion without just grounds or before obtaining sufficient knowledge) in the traditional definition of racism unavoidably leads to the conclusion that racism is "stupid." The online Merriam-Webster dictionary defines "stupid" as follows:[29]

> 1   a: given to unintelligent decisions or acts : acting in an unintelligent or careless manner
>
>   b: lacking intelligence or reason
>
>   ...
>
> 3 :   marked by or resulting from unreasoned thinking or acting.

A racist is defined as having a "prejudiced belief," i.e. a belief developed before considering the facts. There is, of course, no factual basis to believe that an individual's "traits and capacities" are determined by their race. Acting contrary to or in ignorance of the relevant facts clearly is "unintelligent or careless" and certainly "unreasoned." The term "stupid" aptly applies to "racism" and "racists" under the traditional definition.

The **new definition** of racism does not lead to a judgment that racism and racists are "stupid." Although the new definition refers to "prejudice" in the pseudo-mathematical formula "prejudice + power = racism," the element of power necessitates a collective approach because "power" is the presumed ability of one ethnic group (i.e. Whites) to control other ethnic groups. Ascribing "stupid" to an individual makes sense if that person displays racial prejudice, but stating that the supposedly dominant race is stupid and judging all members of that race to be stupid is just as flawed as attributing collective guilt to "Whites."

Only in the United States of America? Changes over time?

The **traditional definition** readily applies not just to individuals in the USA but throughout the world and throughout history. Nazis were blatantly racist. Indeed, racism was a cornerstone of Nazi ideology. Supporters of apartheid in South Africa were blatantly racist. The Armenian Genocide in the early twentieth century was the result of racism. The Rwandan genocide in 1994, when the Hutus slaughtered Tutsis, is a more recent example. Human history going back to ancient Greece and Rome shows that racism, i.e. ethnic prejudice, has existed quite possibly since humans existed.[30]

The **new definition** makes "power" the determinative element. The logical consequence of the new definition is that people cannot be racists unless the ethnic group they belong to has "power." This leads to absurd results. Nazis would not have been racist until Hitler seized power in 1933 because they had no power until then. Did Nazis who survived World War II suddenly stop being racists when Germany surrendered in May 1945? Did the supporters of apartheid cease being racists when power changed in South Africa from the white minority to the black majority or when Robert Mugabe took control in Zimbabwe? The imperial Japanese forces were certainly racist under the new definition during the "Rape of Nanking" at the end of 1937, where prejudice and power combined in one of the most infamous massacres in the 20th century. Did the Japanese military leaders responsible for the slaughter, such as the commander General Iwane Matsui who ordered the massacre and was executed in 1948,[31] stop being racists when Japan surrendered at the end of World War II? Did the Hutus stop being racists when they were driven from power?

What about Jews and Israel? Jews have been victims of ethnic hatred for millennia. Jews are still minorities in all countries of the world except Israel, where they constitute the majority. Upon applying the new definition of racism, Jews cannot be racist except in Israel (and possibly the USA if Jews are lumped in with "whites"), while in Israel, all Jews, as the ethnic group in power in that nation, would be racists under the new definition.

Can members of an ethnic minority be racists?

Anyone can be considered a racist under the **traditional definition** if they have racial prejudice. Louis Farrakhan, the leader of the Black Muslim faith for more than 30 years, is notorious for his countless statements against Jews and white people.[32] "White people are potential human beings...they haven't evolved yet,"[33] is a blatantly racist statement under the traditional definition. Such displays of racial prejudice are commonly referred to as "reverse racism." The position taken by many in academia, according to which all "Whites" are inherently racist, is an example of "reverse racism" under the traditional definition.

Under the **new definition**, Louis Farrakhan's statement is only considered to be an expression of racial prejudice but not racism because he is black. "People of color" cannot be racist under the new definition because they lack "power," an essential element of the new definition.[34] Therefore, Louis Farrakhan, by definition, cannot be a "racist." The proponents of the new definition simply deny that "reverse racism" exists.

> REVERSE RACISM: A term created and used by white people to deny their white privilege. Those in denial use the term reverse racism to refer to hostile behavior by people of color toward Whites and to affirmative action policies, which allegedly give 'preferential treatment' to people of color over Whites. In the U.S., there is no such thing as 'reverse racism.[35]

Situational context and "systemic racism"

Civil rights legislation and case law effectively eliminated all racial discrimination in American law as well as in commercial dealings between private parties more than two generations ago. The impact of historic discrimination could not be quickly eliminated by just rendering racial discrimination illegal, and the War on Poverty, various welfare programs, bussing and affirmative action, and countless other initiatives were implemented to alleviate the effects of past discrimination. Racism under the **traditional**

definition ceased to exist in the American legal and socio-economic system when prejudiced conduct was outlawed.

However, there were still major disparities between ethnic groups in the United States in various respects which continue up to the present day, such as average family income, incarceration rates, health, etc. The **new definition** has been developed and nurtured in American academia for the last 50 years as a tool to explain the fact of continuing socio-economic disparities between "Whites" and "Blacks" or "people of color," especially because the consequence of the individualist approach under the traditional definition of racism is that individuals are primarily responsible for their own successes and failures after race-based discrimination was effectively eliminated.

The proponents of the **new definition** have identified the amorphous concept of "power" as an overarching element to explain the continuing social-economic disparities between ethnic groups. The new definition is also the cornerstone for the concept of **systemic racism** (also referred to as "institutionalized racism"). "Systemic racism" expressly relates to the general situation in which black Americans live in this country. "*Systemic racism* is about everyday experience."[36] One of the main fathers of the concept of "systemic racism" Joe R. Feagin defines "systemic racism" in his foundational work *Racist America* as follows:

> Systemic racism includes the complex array of antiblack [*sic*] practices, the unjustly gained political-economic power of Whites, the continuing economic and other resource inequalities along racial lines, and the white racist ideologies and attitudes created to maintain and rationalize white privilege and power. Systemic here means that the core racist realities are manifested in [...] each major part of U.S. society — the economy, politics, education, religion,

the family—reflects the fundamental reality of systemic racism.[37]

The element "systemic" in the term "systemic racism" is, in effect, identical to the element "power" in the new definition of racism. The inherent link between the term "systemic racism" and the new definition of "racism" as well as the incompatibility with the traditional definition, is readily apparent in the paragraph which immediately follows the previous Feagin quote in which Feagin furthermore equates "white" to being an oppressor:

> There is a tendency on the part of many Americans, especially white Americans, to see racism as an individual matter, as something only outspoken white bigots engage in. Yet racism is much more that [*sic*] an individual matter. It is both individual and systemic. Indeed, systemic racism is perpetuated by a broad social reproduction process that generates not only recurring patterns of discrimination within institutions and by individuals but also an alienating racist relationship – on the one hand, the racially oppressed and, on the other hand, the racial oppressors. [...] It is part of the nature of being positioned as 'white' to be an oppressor, and it is part of the nature of being positioned as "black" to resist oppression.[38]

"Systemic racism" does not presently exist when the **traditional definition** of "racism" is applied. Racial prejudice (i.e. "racism" in the traditional sense) can only be systemic if (i) the system is designed to reflect racial bias, which has not been the case since the civil rights legislation in the 1960s,[39] or if (ii) the system is controlled by individuals who act with racial bias, which is also not the case in modern America unless the political, economic and cultural elites are all considered to be racially prejudiced.

What does racism look like in reality?

Racism, in the **traditional definition,** is relatively easy to identify and sanction. The use of racial epithets or racial bias when dealing with others directly affects the victims of such conduct; they then easily recognize the racist act and the person committing the act.

"**Systemic racism**" is much harder to identify because acts by individuals are not relevant. "Systemic racism" is instead identified on the basis of general socio-economic disparities between races, i.e. a collectivist approach. The American justice system is considered by the proponents of the new definition to be one major area of "systemic racism" since virtually all crime statistics show that Blacks are much more likely to become involved with the American criminal justice system; the proponents of CRT virtually ignore the various reasons for this.[40] Financial disparities, such as home ownership, the wealth gap, and unemployment rates, are also considered to be examples of systemic racism.[41] Even the higher death rate among black Americans from the Wuhan virus (COVID-19) is viewed as an example of "systemic racism."[42]

High crime rates, poverty, poor school performance etc. used to be called "social problems." Under the **new definition** of "racism," social problems are now identical to "systemic racism." The result after considering the collective attribution of fault under the new definition is the following syllogism:

> Proposition 1: "Whites" bear the guilt for systemic racism.
>
> Proposition 2: "Systemic racism is identical to social problems.
>
> Conclusion: Therefore, "Whites" bear the guilt for social problems.

Since the doctrine of "systemic racism" ascribes collective fault along racial lines, the modern concept of "systemic racism" is itself racist under the traditional definition of the term "racism"; it necessarily results in broad condemnation of the entire American society and the majority ethnic group that supposedly controls society. Furthermore, this line of argument distracts from the root causes of various social problems while implying that the black community can do nothing to address social problems until the system is replaced. This reasoning also provides an excuse for criminal activity such as looting.

> I don't care if somebody decides to loot a Gucci or a Macy's or a Nike store because that makes sure that person eats. That makes sure that person has clothes. That is reparations. Anything they want to take, take it because these businesses have insurance.[43]

Consequences of the different definitions for social policy and legislation

The civil rights movement of the 1950s and 1960s reflected the **traditional definition** of racism and resulted in civil rights legislation and aggressive enforcement of these laws. Racial discrimination in the traditional sense is now rare and immediately sanctioned in both American culture as well as law. The way to alleviate socio-economic disparities between ethnic groups is considered to be a long-term process in which individuals earn their way up the socioeconomic ladder with hard work and by making good decisions (e.g. deciding to work hard in school, not joining criminal gangs, not taking illegal drugs, etc.).

The **new definition** places blame on a "system" supposedly controlled by the dominant ethnic group. Failure to prosper is explained by "systemic racism" and not individual shortcomings. Fundamental rules for individual success, such as "self-reliance," the "nuclear family," "emphasis on the scientific method," "Protestant work ethic," "Be polite," etc. have been besmirched as "White Culture." The National Museum of African American History & Culture ("NMAAHC"), part of the Smithsonian, published a chart listing these and other "Aspects of White Culture" in 2020.[44] The NMAAHC subsequently took down this document on the website and apologized for having said that hard work, rational thought etc. are white culture.[45] However, the chart still reflects an apparently widely held view at the NMAAHC because the chart was certainly created and reviewed by many people at the NMAAHC before getting posted on the website.

The new definition of racism especially enables the proponents of "systemic racism" to avoid having to look at more complex explanations for socio-economic disparities. Instead, blame is placed on the "system." Aggression is directed toward representatives of the system, such as law enforcement personnel. The symbols of the "system," such as the flag and statues of historic figures, are dishonored and vandalized.

The new definition also leads to demands for solutions that superficially treat the symptoms of social problems. For example, the demand for reparations is intended to address the wealth gap by simply transferring money from white Americans to black Americans. The suggestion for dealing with higher incarceration rates is to simply release black prisoners and gut the justice system. These demands and other common demands in the Black Lives Matter ("BLM") movement are directed towards creating equal socio-economic results for black and white Americans by edict without attending to the underlying causes of the disparities. The BLM movement is very decentralized and currently (2023) undergoing major changes. Local BLM organizations have somewhat different demands. BLM Seattle, for example, defunding the police, an end to cash bail, and an end to youth incarceration, among many other demands.[46]

Such superficial solutions can be as mundane as the Affirmatively Furthering Fair Housing Rule adopted in the Obama administration, under which local zoning laws, for example, would have to permit the construction of low-cost apartments in neighborhoods otherwise zoned for single-family residences for the purpose of evening out demographic differences between neighborhoods.[47] This rule is a logical consequence of the new definition because it is intended to counter the fact that economic disparities between Whites and People of Color naturally result in a higher percentage of ethnic minorities living in apartment buildings and public housing and a higher percentage of "Whites" living in neighborhoods zoned for single-family dwellings. This rule, however, does not address the underlying economic reasons for people living in different neighborhoods. Under the traditional definition, there is no "racial bias" if the decision about who lives in the neighborhood results from the ability of the individual to pay for a home. Under the new definition, the mere fact of different ethnic mixes between high-income and low-income neighborhoods is an expression of "systemic racism."[48]

The differences between the traditional definition of racism and the new definition developed in academia are perhaps most easily seen in criminal law and policy. For example, 6,380 black Americans were arrested in 2018 for "murder and nonnegligent [sic] manslaughter," while 5,280 Whites (including Hispanics) were arrested in 2018 for the same offense.[49] Black Americans constitute only 13.4% of the population, while Whites (without Hispanics) amount to 60.1% (76.3% with Hispanics who are also considered to be white for the purpose of many crime statistics).[50] This means that Blacks are arrested for criminal homicide at a roughly five times greater rate. The traditional definition of racism provides no explanation for these statistics since there is no indication that arrests of Blacks are based on racial prejudice. The causes for the different rates, when considering the **traditional definition**, must be found elsewhere, e.g. in socio-economic and cultural causes, such as the gangster sub-culture, poverty, poor education, growing up in homes without a father, etc.

Under the **new definition**, the cause is necessarily attributed to "systemic racism." Therefore, policies to lower the homicide rate among black Americans by addressing the causes of the high homicide rate will be determined differently, depending on the definition that is applied. Policies reflecting the traditional definition will address socio-economic factors and culture, while policies reflecting the new definition will confront the "system" as the source of "systemic racism" and look for quick fixes to eliminate statistical disparities.

The "advantage" of the new definition and the related concept of "systemic racism" compared to the traditional definition is that the new definition makes it a lot easier to place blame for socio-economic disparities while absolving the individual of personal responsibility. The **new definition** just blames the entire legal and social system, cries "racism" and rails against the "system." For example, if there is a high crime rate in a black neighborhood which results in increased police contact with the local population, the analysis under "systemic racism" will challenge the justice system and call for such actions as defunding the police. The result is what we see now in major American cities in which crime rates go up while effective law enforcement goes down.

Proponents of the **traditional definition** look to the underlying socio-economic causes and, for example, strengthen police presence in high-crime neighborhoods. The approach under the traditional definition is accordingly directed towards addressing specific problems rather than ranting against the "system" and trying to tear it down.

"Systemic racism" is an example of sophistry promulgated by well-paid academics as an essentially simplistic means of explaining socio-economic disparities among racial groups in the USA. The concept of "systemic racism" and the new definition of the term "racism" are tailored to the political situation in the USA and lead to absurd results when applied to history and other nations. "Systemic racism" is based on a definition of racism that downplays or even eliminates the aspect of individual racial prejudice and instead uses a collectivist approach to ascribe collective guilt ("All Whites are racist.") and collective innocence ("Blacks cannot be racist."). The concept of "systemic racism" categorizes people as "oppressors" (all white Americans) and those who "resist oppression" (all people of color, especially black Americans). This divides the country and easily leads to violence directed against the "system." Finally, the concept of "systemic racism" leads to simplistic public policies that focus on treating the symptoms (e.g. releasing incarcerated Blacks) rather than the cause (e.g. combatting criminal gangs and encouraging the local community to snitch on criminals). The academic world has used intellectual sleight-of-hand to create a new definition of racism and the concept of "systemic racism."

The concept of "systemic racism" recently triggered major riots in American cities following the death of George Floyd. The rioters and the protestors giving them cover are convinced that they are combatting the evils of "racism" by attacking the "system," i.e. their own country and fellow Americans. Innocent people have lost their businesses and even their lives in the riots. Law and order have almost completely broken down in many American cities. The new definition of racism and the concept of "systemic racism" have been used to justify destroying our country. The resulting damage to peace and prosperity is completely unacceptable. The only people who have profited from the new definition of "racism" in CRT and the corresponding, intellectually vacuous "systemic racism" are the countless academicians, authors, and "diversity consultants" who make excellent livings from selling such tripe. It is time to relegate the concept of "systemic racism" to the repository of obsolete academic doctrines. Finally, it is time for all Americans to address social problems such as rising crime rates honestly and with resolve without having to bear a cross of collective guilt.

Chapter Summary

Clearly defined terms are essential for rational communication. That is why fundamental terms are expressly defined in contracts and statutes. Therefore, understanding Critical Race Theory requires a clear understanding of the terms "race" and "racism." The CRT definition of "race" as a "social construct" is generally consistent with the traditional understanding of "race." The term "racism" is traditionally understood to mean racial prejudice, i.e. judging someone or a group by their "race." Critical Race Theory redefines "racism" to mean "racial prejudice + power." This new definition deserves rejection and condemnation for numerous reasons: The new definition fails to recognize individual responsibility for being a "racist" (in the traditional sense of the term). The concept of "power" in the new definition is equivalent to the "oppressor-oppressed" dialectic in Critical Race Theory, and "race" is the relevant criterion for determining who supposedly has "power" and is, thus, the "oppressor." Finally, the new definition of racism assigns collective and generational guilt based on "race." This group condemnation is itself racist under the traditional definition.

---

[1]   This chapter is based in large part on an article I wrote in August 2020 in response to the constant refrain in the press and among especially liberal politicians after the killing of George Floyd in May 2020 that the United States is a "systemically racist" country. The article was published online in CalCoast News at https://calcoastnews.com/2020/09/the-myth-of-systemic-racism/.

[2]   Tim Wise, "Oops, Your denial of Systemic Racism Sorta Proves Systemic Racism". The Good Men Project (November 22, 2022), at https://goodmenproject.com/featured-content/oops-your-denial-of-systemic-racism-sorta-proves-systemic-racism/.

[3]   While conducting the research for the original 2020 article, I found a similar analysis of the different definitions of "racism" in an article by B.J. Campbell "The Two Confusing Definitions of Racism" originally published in Medium.com (August 26, 2018), available at https://hwfo.substack.com/p/the-two-confusing-definitions-of.

[4]   https://www.webster-dictionary.org/definition/racism.

[5]   https://www.webster-dictionary.org/definition/racist.

[6]   https://www.merriam-webster.com/dictionary/race; The word "race" has many meanings having nothing to do with ethnicity such as a competition for speed or a flowing body of water.

[7]   https://www.azquotes.com/quote/1146287.

[8]   https://www.youtube.com/watch?v=SMy08ygVdLA, triggering quite a controversy at the time https://www.npr.org/sections/codeswitch/2014/04/01/297862152/in-cancelcolbert-a-firestorm-and-a-lost-opportunity.

[9]   Delgado/Stefancic, pg. 9.

[10]   Ibram X. Kendi, How to be an Antiracist, (2019), pg. 60.

[11]   https://www.merriam-webster.com/dictionary/prejudice.

[12.]   Nicki Lisa Cole, Ph.D., "Defining Racism Beyond its Dictionary Meaning: A System of Power, Privilege, and Oppression", published at ThoughtCo., last updated 14 July 2019, https://www.thoughtco.com/racism-definition-3026511.

[13]   Caleb Rosado, Dept. of Urban Studies Eastern University Philadelphia, PA, "The Undergirding Factor is POWER, Toward an

Understanding of Prejudice and Racism", EdChange.org, http://www.edchange.org/multicultural/papers/caleb/racism.html.

14   William Voegeli, "Racism Revised, The way we hate now" in Claremont Review of Books, Fall 2018, https://claremontreviewofbooks.com/racism-revised/.

15   Linda McKay-Pano, "The Importance of Distinguishing Racism from Racial Discrimination", Alberta Civil Liberties Research Centre (September 8, 2020), https://www.aclrc.com/blog/2020/9/8/the-importance-of-distinguishing-racism-from-racial-discrimination.

16   Caleb Rosado, ibid. footnote 13, at http://www.edchange.org/multicultural/papers/caleb/racism.html.

17   "Merriam-Webster Revises 'Racism' Entry After Missouri Woman Asks for Changes", New York Times, June 10, 2020, at https://www.nytimes.com/2020/06/10/us/merriam-webster-racism-definition.html.

18   Robin DiAngelo, *White Fragility*, Beacon Press (2018), pg. 20, at https://www.google.com/books/edition/White_Fragility/ZfQ3DwAAQBAJ?hl=en&gbpv=1&printsec=frontcover.

19   E. Tammy Kim, "The Perils of 'People of Color' ", The New Yorker, July 29, 2020, https://www.newyorker.com/news/annals-of-activism/the-perils-of-people-of-color.

20   Robin DiAngelo, *White Fragility*, pg. 1.

21   "Definitions and Descriptions of Racism", University of Iowa Wiki service, at https://wiki.uiowa.edu/download/attachments/31756797/Racism+-Definitions+.pdf.

22   E.A. Gjelten, "Does the First Amendment Protect Hate Speech?", updated March 22, 2019, https://www.lawyers.com/legal-info/criminal/does-the-first-amendment-protect-hate-speech.html.

23   "Man charged with making 'racist or anti-religious' Facebook comments about British soldier's death", Daily Mail, May 24, 2013, updated May 25, 2013, https://www.dailymail.co.uk/news/article-2330180/Woolwich-attacks-Man-charged-making-racist-anti-religious-Facebook-comments-British-soldier-s-death.html.

24   English version: https://www.gesetze-im-internet.de/englisch_stgb/englisch_stgb.html#p1333.

25   The Golden Rule, Internet Encyclopedia of Philosophy, https://iep.utm.edu/goldrule/.

26   "I have a dream" speech on August 28, 1963 in Washington, D.C., full text at https://www.aol.com/article/news/2017/01/16/dr-martin-luther-kings-i-have-a-dream-speech-full-text/21655947/.

27   Quoted by Dustin Dwyer, "Why all white people are racist, but can't handle being called racist: the theory of white fragility", Michigan Radio (March 15, 2015), https://stateofopportunity.michiganradio.org/post/why-all-white-people-are-racist-cant-handle-being-called-racist-theory-white-fragility.

28   Ibid., footnote 25.

29   https://www.merriam-webster.com/dictionary/stupid.

30   A large list can be found in Wikipedia, https://en.wikipedia.org/wiki/Genocides_in_history; see also Benjamin Isaac, *The Invention of Racism in Classical Antiquity*, Princeton University Press (2006).

31   Wikipedia, https://en.wikipedia.org/wiki/Iwane_Matsui.

32   "Farrakhan: In his own words", https://www.adl.org/education/resources/reports/nation-of-islam-farrakhan-in-his-own-words.

33   Ibid., citing Philadelphia Inquirer (March 18, 2000).

34   Michael Gao, "Who Can Be 'Racist'?" The Harvard Crimson (August 10, 2018), https://www.thecrimson.com/column/between-the-lines/article/2018/8/10/gao-who-can-be-racist/.

35   Keith Lawrence and Terry Keleher, "Structural Racism", paper prepared for the Race and Public Policy Conference 2004, https://www.intergroupresources.com/rc/Definitions%20of%20Racism.pdf.

36   Joe R. Feagin, *Racist America*, Routledge (2001), pg. 4, available online at https://books.google.com/books?id=vwHxti-rSYgC&printsec=frontcover#v=onepage&q&f=false.

37   Ibid. pg. 6.

38   Ibid. pg. 6.

39   Case law has countered even implicit bias in laws and regulations as well as business practice under the concept of "disparate impact" (see e.g. Griggs v. Duke Power Co., 401 U.S. 424 (1974), available at https://www.law.cornell.edu/supremecourt/text/401/424.

40   Bill Quigley, "Fourteen Examples of Systemic Racism in the US Criminal Justice System", published in Common Dreams (July 26, 2010, available at

https://www.commondreams.org/views/2010/07/26/fourteen-examples-systemic-racism-us-criminal-justice-system.

[41] Angela Hanks, Danyelle Solomon, Christian Weller, "Systemic Inequality – How America's Structural Racism Helped Create the Black-White Wealth Gap", published at americanprogress.org (February 21, 2018), https://www.americanprogress.org/issues/race/reports/2018/02/21/4470 51/systematic-inequality/.

[42] "Health Equity Considerations and Racial and Ethnic Minority Groups", National Center for Immunization and Respiratory Diseases (U.S.), Division of Viral Diseases (July 24, 2020), https://stacks.cdc.gov/view/cdc/91049.

[43] Statement by Ariel Atkins, quoted in the article "Reparations are about economic stability, not a looted pair of $120 Nikes" by Dahleen Glanton, The Chicago Tribune", August 17, 2020 https://www.chicagotribune.com/columns/dahleen-glanton/ct-looting-black-lives-matter-reparataions-20200817-xdxu4ipu5rhqzkbdl4fpslsnha-story.html.

[44] Reproduced in the article by Marina Watts, "In Smithsonian Race Guidelines, Rational Thinking and Hard Work Are White Values", Newsweek (July 1, 2020), https://www.newsweek.com/smithsonian-race-guidelines-rational-thinking-hard-work-are-white-values-1518333.

[45] Chacour Koop, "Smithsonian museum apologizes for saying hard work, rational though is 'white culture' ", Miami Herald (July 17, 2020), https://www.miamiherald.com/news/nation-world/national/article244309587.html.

[46] Black Lives Matter - Seattle - King County, https://blacklivesseattle.org/our-demands/.

[47] Handel Destinvil, "Obama Administration Introduces New Affirmative Rule on Fair Housing", American Bar Association (August 13, 2015), https://www.americanbar.org/groups/litigation/committees/minority-trial-lawyer/practice/2015/obama-administration-introduces-new-administrative-rule-fair-housing/.

[48] Danielle Kurtzleben, "Seeking Suburban Votes, Trump to Repeal Rule Combating Racial Bias in Housing", NPR (July 21, 2020), https://www.npr.org/2020/07/21/893471887/seeking-suburban-votes-trump-targets-rule-to-combat-racial-bias-in-housing.

[49] U.S. Department of Justice, Office of Juvenile Justice and Delinquency Prevention, Estimated number of arrests by offense and

race, 2018, All Ages,
https://www.ojjdp.gov/ojstatbb/crime/ucr.asp?table_in=2.
[50]   United States Census Bureau Quick Facts,
https://www.census.gov/quickfacts/fact/table/US/PST045219.

Chapter IV

Basic Tenets of Critical Race Theory

An ideology is built on a few fundamental principles (assumptions). In addition to redefining "race" as purely a social construct and "racism" as "racial prejudice + power", the foundational premises of Critical Race Theory are the following:

1. Racism is ubiquitous, i.e. "racism is ordinary, not aberrational – 'normal science,' the usual way society does business, the common, everyday experience of most people of color in this country."[1]

2. Advances in the law benefiting or harming minorities tend to occur when they serve the interests of the dominant white elites and working-class Whites (so-called "interest convergence" or "material determinism").[2]

3. The thesis of race as a "social construct" states that race is a product of social thought and relations and that race is not "objective, inherent or fixed" and that race does not correspond to any "biological or genetic reality."[3]

4. "Differential racialization," according to which "[T]he dominant society racializes different minority groups at different times, in response to shifting needs such as the labor market."[4] This concept is closely tied to the social construct thesis and addresses the supposed motivation for a white-dominated society to delineate (and oppress) other races.

5. "Intersectionality" and "anti-essentialism" are terms for a concept developed by Kimberlé Crenshaw in 1989.[5] These ever-so intellectually sounding terms

refer to the obvious fact that individuals have various characteristics, and these characteristics can overlap.

6. The "voice of color thesis" argues that "[m]inority status ... brings with it a presumed competence to speak about race and racism."[6]

7. "Storytelling" is an essential aspect of Critical Race Theory[7] and is sometimes referred to as "counter-storytelling."[8] Storytelling is not a substantive tenet of CRT, but it is a basic tactic in pursuing the ideological goals of CRT by using emotion-laden, individual stories to motivate people to take action in furtherance of the ideological goals of CRT.

These principles are derived from the dialectical nature of critical theory and reflect the intellectually simple, binary splitting of society into the oppressed class and the oppressor class. The definitional artifices discussed in the previous section, with their inherent focus on groups while ignoring individualism, have resulted in an ideology that is contrary to the principles upon which the American constitutional republic has been established. At the same time, Critical Race Theory distracts from real solutions for real social problems and instead has led to a CRT "industry" that exploits "white guilt" and costs our country billions of dollars every year while benefiting a new generation of race hustlers.

The following sections examine the basic tenets of Critical Race Theory as well the concept of storytelling.

1. The main tenet: Racism is ordinary, the usual way society does business

Much of the criticism directed against Critical Race Theory is based on the argument that CRT looks at everything through the lens of race: "The idea they're teaching is to examine everything through the lens of race, and that is very worrisome."[9] Proponents of CRT agree.[10] Regardless of whether the subject is history, medicine, crime, or socio-economic disparities between ethnic groups, "racism" is viewed as the underlying factor. This makes sense under the primary tenet of CRT, according to which "racism is ordinary, the usual way society does business." CRT scholars accept this tenet without question because this is the most fundamental premise of the CRT ideology. Raising doubts about this premise casts doubt on the viability of the entire CRT ideology.

Racism in the traditional sense has obviously been present in the United States and, for that matter, the rest of the world throughout human history. The degree to which racism played a role in historical events and the development of social structures has varied over the course of time and from place to place. The proponents of CRT, however, characterize racism as something invented specifically by white Europeans in the 1600s, especially in connection with the colonization and development of North America.[11] "Chattel slavery," under which a slave is considered to be the property of the slave owner, is sometimes believed to have been unique to America. This is wrong; chattel slavery has existed at various times and in various societies throughout human history.[12]

Many other factors have also been of great significance in the development of the United States and the rest of the world. For example, the Industrial Revolution reshaped all human existence and was driven by advancements in technology. The Age of Discovery (15th to 18th century) was motivated by economics and the desire for more efficient trade with Asia. The Reformation, which began in 1517 when Martin Luther published his "Disputation on the Power of Indulgences" (the 95 Theses[13]), and later the Thirty Years' War (1618 – 1648) decisively altered the face of Europe, but these events had nothing to do with race and instead involved religion. Maximizing the relevance of race when studying history or analyzing societal problems while minimizing other factors is myopic in the extreme.

Of course, racial prejudice is one of many important factors that have played a major role in how African-Americans and individuals in other ethnic groups have been treated, especially historically, by the law and their fellow citizens. Prejudice, i.e. "an adverse opinion or leaning formed without just grounds or before sufficient knowledge" has also affected other groups such as women, homosexuals, the elderly ("ageism"), and others from the time the United States was established. It took almost 200 years for the promise of individual liberty embodied in the Declaration of Independence and the Constitution to finally become reality in American law for all people in America.

The civil rights movement in the middle of the 20th century culminated in a process that eliminated the last vestiges of racial discrimination in American law. Laws and regulations based on racial prejudice have not been in effect in the United States for approximately two generations. Racial prejudice in private economic dealings between individuals has also been outlawed for two generations. Anyone who today shows racial or other prejudice in employment, housing, and business, in general, is subject to severe sanctions in the form of penalties and civil damages.

The developments in the last two generations belie the fundamental premise of Critical Race Theory. This is readily apparent upon a brief review of civil rights legislation in the United States. At the Federal level, the first Civil Rights Act was passed in 1866 following the adoption of the 13th Amendment in January 1865, which abolished slavery, and before the adoption of the 14th Amendment in 1868, which codified the concept of equal protection under the law.

However, neither the constitutional amendments nor the Civil Rights Act of 1866 prevented racial discrimination both in fact and under "Jim Crow" laws which were upheld under the "separate but equal" doctrine established by the US Supreme Court in the infamous *Plessy v. Ferguson* decision of 1896.

The years after the end of World War II saw the desegregation of the armed forces of the United States start with Executive Order 9981 issued by President Harry Truman on 26 July 1948.[14] The Army started integrating units during the Korean War, and racial segregation in all branches of the armed forces ended on 30 September 1954 when the Secretary of Defense announced that all-black military units had been abolished.[15] President Truman also issued Executive Order 9980 on 26 July 1948 that eliminated discrimination based on "race, color, religion, or national origin" in the Federal workforce.[16]

Desegregation in education started in 1954 with the US Supreme Court's decision in *Brown v. Board of Education of Topeka*, 347 U.S. 483,[17] which in effect, eliminated the "separate but equal" doctrine that had been adopted in *Plessy v. Ferguson*. The Supreme Court, concerned about efforts in the South to slow-walk desegregation of schools, issued an order in 1955 to admit students "to public schools on a racially nondiscriminatory basis with all deliberate speed."[18] Desegregation of public schools was still being resisted, especially in southern states. Governor Orval Faubus of Arkansas was particularly stubborn, and President Eisenhower sent the 101st Airborne Division to enforce desegregation at Central High School in Little Rock by escorting the "Little Rock Nine" students into the school in defiance of racist protesters.

Individual states also adopted civil rights laws to prohibit discrimination on the basis of race and other factors.

California adopted the Unruh Civil Rights Act in 1959, which has been amended, in the meantime, to include more protected classes.[19] The state of Washington adopted the "Law Against Discrimination in Employment" ten years earlier, in 1949.[20] The state of New York has a long history of civil rights legislation going back to March of 1945 when the Ives-Quinn Anti-Discrimination Act was adopted and signed by Governor Thomas Dewey.[21] Contrary to the efforts of the Federal Government in the years after World War II, this state legislation provided broad protection against racial discrimination in private dealings, e.g. employment.

The Federal Government followed suit with the Civil Rights Act of 1964, which established broad protection against racial discrimination in the private sector. This statute was followed by further civil rights legislation, such as the Civil Rights Act of 1965, which addressed voter discrimination, the Fair Housing Act of 1968, and the Equal Employment Opportunity Act of 1972. Anti-discrimination laws in the United States also created the template for anti-discrimination laws in the rest of the world. Australia adopted anti-discrimination laws starting in 1975 with the Racial Discrimination Act 1975. The Race Relations Act was adopted in Great Britain in 1965. Germany adopted the General Ani-discrimination Act (*Allgemeines Gleichbehandlungsgesetz*) in 2006, although case law had previously provided significant protection, particularly in the area of employment. The European Union adopted the Race Equality Directive 200/43/EC in 2000.

Furthermore, the American anti-discrimination laws have been vigorously enforced since they were adopted by both governmental agencies such as the Equal Employment Opportunity Commission ("EEOC") as well as in private litigation. Discrimination in violation of civil rights legislation has been subject to severe penalties as well as large claims for damages for a half-century now.

The fact that racism (in the traditional meaning of the term) has been prohibited by law throughout the United States for at least two generations accordingly begs the question:

Where is all the racism that the primary tenet of CRT assumes to exist today?

How many racist acts (in the traditional sense of the term "racist") have you committed today or last week or last year, or ever? How many racist acts have members of your family or friends committed? When was the last time you even thought about telling an ethnic joke, such as "How many [*insert any ethnic group*] does it take to change a light bulb?" When was the last time you even witnessed a racist act? There are, of course, always individuals of every race who are so stupid that they focus on other individuals' ethnicity and are unwilling or unable to judge someone by their character and not the color of their skin. However, stupid behavior on the part of a few individuals does not, by any stretch of the imagination, come close to being "ordinary, the usual way society does business."

No matter: The proponents of CRT have a ready answer. Since conscious racial bias is hard to find, the answer must be that Whites have **unconscious bias**, i.e. "[r]acism that operates at an unconscious or subtle level,"[22] also called "**implicit racial bias**" which is defined as follows:

> It is important to distinguish implicit racial bias from racism or discrimination. Implicit biases are associations made by individuals in the unconscious state of mind. This means that the individual is likely not aware of the biased association.

Implicit racial bias can cause individuals to unknowingly act in discriminatory ways. This does not mean that the individual is overtly racist, but rather that their perceptions have been shaped by experiences, and these perceptions potentially result in biased thoughts or actions.

No one is immune from having unconscious thoughts and associations, but becoming aware of implicit racial bias creates an avenue for addressing the issue.[23]

Unconscious (implicit) bias is, by definition, intangible. People supposedly afflicted with unconscious bias aren't even aware that they have it. Therefore, the only way to identify unconscious bias is to search for the alleged effects of unconscious bias. There have been numerous studies that attempt to identify employment discrimination resulting from unconscious bias. The findings of many studies, as summarized in a lead study in New York City in 2009, "Discrimination in a Low-Wage Labor Market: A Field Experiment,"[24] are at best ambiguous.

A series of studies relying on surveys and in-depth interviews finds that firms are reluctant to hire young minority men, - especially African Americans - because they are seen as unreliable, dishonest, or lacking in social or cognitive skills (Waldinger and Lichter 2003; Moss and Tilly 2001; Holzer 1996; Kirschenman & Neckerman, 1991; Wilson 1996, chap. 5). The strong negative attitudes expressed by employers suggest that race remains highly salient in employers' evaluations of workers. At the same time, however, research relying on interviews with employers leaves uncertain the degree to which self-reported attitudes are reflected in actual hiring decisions (Pager & Quillian, 2005).

Indeed, Philip Moss and Chris Tilly (2001) report the puzzling finding that "businesses, where a plurality of managers complained about black motivation, are more likely to hire black men" (p.151). In fact, across a series of analyses controlling for firm size, starting wage, the percent black in the relevant portion of the metropolitan area, and the business' average distance from black residents in the area, the authors find that employers who overtly criticize the hard skills or interaction skills of black workers are between two and four times more likely to hire a black worker (p.151-152). Hiring decisions are influenced by a complex range of factors, racial attitudes being only one. The stated preferences of employers, then, leave uncertain the degree to which negative attitudes about Blacks translate into active forms of discrimination.

Indeed, other research focusing on wages rather than employment reports even less evidence of contemporary discrimination. Derek Neal and William Johnson (1996), for example, estimate wage differences between white, black, and Latino young men. They find that two-thirds of the black-white gap in wages in 1990-1991 can be explained by race differences in cognitive test scores measured 11 years earlier; test scores fully explain wage differences between Whites and Latinos. This and similar studies trace the employment problems of young minority men primarily to skill or other individual deficiencies rather than any direct effect of discrimination (Neal and Johnson 1996; Farkas and Vicknair 1996; O'Neill, 1990). Economist James Heckman (1998) puts the point most clearly, writing that "most of the disparity in earnings between Blacks and Whites in the labor market of the 1990s is due to differences in skills they bring to the market, and not to discrimination within the labor market...' He goes on to describe labor market discrimination as "the problem of an earlier era' (Heckman, 1998:101-102).[25]

This 2009 "Field Experiment" used teams consisting of three testers, one black, one white, and one Latino, with equivalent qualifications who applied for entry-level jobs in New York City. The study showed preferential treatment of Whites over both Latinos and Blacks and preferential treatment of Latinos over Blacks. This discrimination expressed itself in the forms of (i) "categorical exclusion" in 5 of 47 cases, i.e. the most severe form of discrimination involving immediate rejection with virtually no consideration given to the application,[26] (ii) "shifting standards," i.e. failing to apply hiring standards in a uniform manner, and (iii) "job channeling," i.e. guiding an applicant away from the originally intended job to another job with either better status ("upward channeling" or lower status ("downward channeling"). The discrimination was mostly subtle.

The episodes of discrimination recorded in this study were seldom characterized by overt racism or hostility. In fact, our testers rarely perceived any signs of clear prejudice. It was only through side-by-side comparisons of our testers' experiences that patterns of subtle but consistent differential treatment were revealed. Minority applicants were disqualified more readily or hired more reluctantly than their white partners with identical skills and experience. Additionally, black and Latino applicants were routinely channeled into positions requiring less customer contact and more manual work than their white counterparts. Where we observe interactions between applicants and employers, we see a small number of cases that reflect seemingly rigid racial preferences on the part of employees. More often, differential treatment emerged in the social interaction of the job interview. Employers appeared to see more potential in the stated qualifications of white applicants and more commonly viewed white applicants as a better fit for more desirable jobs.[27]

The authors of the 2009 "Field Experiment" recognized that their findings did not reflect the overall level of discrimination against minority job seekers in New York City. The study also focused on small employers and "the kinds of low-skill service work that dominate low-wage labor markets."[28] The study accordingly provides no input on large employers or applicants for higher-level jobs. One glaring omission in the 2009 "Field Experiment" is that it does not consider the race of the employer or the person at an employer making the hiring decisions.

A more recent study in 2021 looked at large employers from among the Fortune 500 companies.[29] This study examined 108 of the largest U.S. employers by sending 83,000 fictitious applications for jobs posted by the employers and comparing the contacts by employers in response to the applications with "black" names and "white" names. The study also included in the applications various combinations of factors such as membership in clubs "signaling LGBTQ affiliation" or generic clubs (e.g. debate club), preferred pronouns, and implied age over 40.[30] The study found, "Distinctively Black names reduce the probability of employer contact by 2.1 percentage points relative to distinctively white names."[31] The study did not identify widespread discrimination in all companies and instead found discrimination in 23 of the 108 companies.[32]

As was the case with the 2009 "Field Experiment", the study did not consider the race of the person(s) at the company making the decision to contact the applicant. Assuming merely for the sake of argument that all the persons making the hiring decisions in the 2009 and 2021 studies were white, the studies would indicate that they subconsciously prefer other Whites. This begs the question of whether employers of other ethnic groups give preferential treatment to members of their own groups. There has apparently been only one major study about this subject, "Why Are Black Employers More Likely than White Employers to Hire Blacks?"[33] This study found that black employers are more likely to hire Blacks than white employers for several reasons, including (i) "[t]he black application rate is much higher at firms with black than white employers," (ii) black employers discriminate less against black applicants than white employers, (iii) a black employer with black customers will favor black job applicants.[34]

The studies in the job market do not show widespread racial discrimination, let alone conscious discrimination. However, the studies indicate that members of one ethnic group may subconsciously prefer someone like them, i.e. in the same ethnic group. It is especially likely that a smaller employer might prefer working with someone like him/her. Just a glance at smaller restaurants serving ethnic food shows that they tend to hire people from their own ethnic group. Chinese restaurants often have a disproportionately high number of Chinese employees. Mexican grocery stores in California often seem to have a disproportionately high number of Hispanic employees. Is that because they are racist businesses?

The "Field Study" of small employers in New York and the recent study of large employers are not directly comparable with each other. Nonetheless, it seems that the incidents and degree of discrimination were less at large employers. This might be a function of the fact that hiring decisions at smaller employers are made by one person, namely, the owner, while multiple persons are often involved in making a hiring decision at a large employer. A comparison study might be an interesting task for a group of sociologists since it appears that there has not yet been any such study comparing hiring practices of small employers with hiring by large employers.

The subconscious preference for members of the same ethnic group is common in private dealings among individuals. People often seek friends and spouses from within their own ethnic groups. However, we do not, for example, consider a person to be a racist just because that individual feels more attracted to a potential spouse who is from the same ethnic group. Nor is a person a racist just because many or even all of that person's personal contacts belong to the same ethnic group.

The fact that studies such as those involving the job market do not show widespread unconscious racial bias throughout society does not end the search for the holy grail of unconscious racism (implicit bias). Indeed, this quest rivals the search in physics for the "God particle," a subatomic particle thought to exist by theoretical physicists in 1964, although they could not actually identify it. The story goes that the physicist Leo Lederman and his co-author Dick Teresi wanted to title a book, *The Goddamn Particle*, but their publisher rejected the title in favor of "The God Particle." The title and name stuck. The particle, now called the "Higgs boson" was finally proven to exist using the Large Hadron Collider in Cern, Switzerland.[35] Searching the unconscious is even more difficult than searching for an infinitesimally small subatomic particle. No piece of equipment, not even the Large Hadron Collider, can prove the existence of conscious thought, let alone something that exists below the level of consciousness.

That has not deterred academicians in the social sciences from trying for over two decades to construct a social science version of the Large Hadron Collider. Perhaps the most well-known attempt is the Implicit Association Test ("IAT"), developed by scholars from leading universities in 1998 and recently updated.[36] The test uses rapid responses to words and images. I took the test on 20 February 2022. The result said that I (white) have a "slight preference for black people." I sent the link to a black friend who is a strong supporter of BLM. His result showed "no automatic preference." My personal reaction to the test was that it strained my eye-finger coordination, which perhaps had some influence on my test result.

The scientific value of the IAT is, at best dubious. Although it was quite popular, with great credence being placed on it, especially around the time Barack Obama was running for president in 2008,[37] substantial doubts about the usefulness of the IAT have arisen, even among the scholars working on the project. People who have spent great parts of their careers developing, refining, and working with the IAT no longer find it reliable in addressing individual behavior.

> The point is that the key experts involved in IAT research no longer claim that the IAT can be used to predict individual behavior. In this sense, the IAT has simply failed to deliver on a promise it has been making since its inception.[38]

Supporters of the IAT have recognized that the IAT is not accurate when applied to an individual.[39] In a recent article published in 2020, leading IAT researchers recognized this criticism and came up with an impressively large list of modifications for improving the IAT and how it is administered.[40]

Socio-economic disparities

Racial discrimination has been struck from the law for two generations. Racism is also not a subconscious plague afflicting "white" America. So where is it? CRT proponents invariably point to socio-economic disparities between ethnic groups as evidence that (systemic) racism exists. The analysis again has a certain similarity to the search for the "God Particle." Just as effects in subatomic physics led scientists to theorize in 1964 about the existence of the Higgs boson, finally proven three decades later, the existence of a wide range of socio-economic disparities leads social scientists to theorize about the existence of racism as the singular cause for the disparities. However, that is where the analogy to the natural sciences meets its limit.

There are now countless studies about socio-economic disparities between ethnic groups.[41] These socio-economic disparities are frequently cited as "examples of systemic racism against black Americans."[42] There are, of course, socio-economic disparities among various ethnic groups, and these disparities exist not just between "Whites" and black Americans. For example, the 2019 Survey of Consumer Finances found that "the typical White family has eight times the wealth of the typical Black family and five times the wealth of the typical Hispanic family."[43] The same survey shows disparities between ethnic groups in home ownership. In both categories of net wealth and home ownership, the survey also shows that the group "Other" is in second place behind "Whites." "Other" consists of people who identify as Asian, American Indian, Alaska Native, Native Hawaiian, or Pacific Islander, people having more than one racial self-identification and other racial identities.

There are also clear disparities among various ethnic groups in education. For example, statistics for U.S. adults over 25 show for 2019 that 40% of "Blacks," 31% of

"Hispanics," 56% of "Whites" and 78% of "Asians" have associate arts degrees.[44] The statistics for "U.S: Adults Over 25 for 2019 show 29% of "Blacks," 21% of "Hispanics," 45% of "Whites" and 71% of "Asians" have bachelor's degrees or higher.[45] Disparities also exist in school discipline in suspensions and expulsions. The school discipline rates for "Blacks" were substantially higher than for "Hispanics and "Whites," and "Asians" had the lowest school discipline rates.[46]

> California's Black students, Black boys in particular, are far more likely than their peers to be suspended or expelled throughout their school career, especially during kindergarten through third grade, a recent study by San Diego State University professors found.[47]

The disparities in crime statistics are especially large and cited as evidence of systemic racism in the American criminal justice system. Out of a total of 16,335 murder offenders in 2019, the race of 11,493 offenders was known. Of this number, 6,425 (55.9%) were "Black," 4,728 (41,1 %) were "White" (this group also includes Hispanics), and 340 (3.0%) were "Other."[48] . The statistics show a similar pattern for nonfatal violent crimes, especially for "Blacks":

> In 2018, based on data from the FBI's Uniform Crime Reporting (UCR) Program, *black people were overrepresented among persons arrested for nonfatal violent* crimes (33%) and for serious nonfatal violent crimes (36%) relative to their representation in the U.S. population (13%) […]. White people were underrepresented. White people accounted for 60% of U.S. residents but 46% of all persons arrested for rape, robbery, aggravated assault, and other assault, and 39% of all arrestees for nonfatal violent crimes excluding other assault.

Hispanics, regardless of their race, were overrepresented among arrestees for nonfatal violent crimes, excluding other assault (21%) relative to their representation in the U.S. population (18%).[49]

The statistics on non-negligent homicides and non-fatal violent crime are reflected in the statistics on incarceration in federal prisons and, in general, in the United States. As of March 22, 2022, the Federal Bureau of Prisons had approximately 150,000 inmates, of which 38.3% were "Black," compared to a total of approximately 13% in the total population. "Whites" (including Hispanics) made up approximately 57.7% of the Federal prison population.[50] The situation is similar in state prisons and jails, with "Blacks" making up approximately 38% of the incarcerated population.[51]

Identifying socio-economic disparities is a fertile and lucrative field for social scientists, not just with regard to various ethnic groups. Socio-economic disparities have been found between obese people and people who are not obese,[52] with the predictable result that "weightism" is viewed as a form of bias.[53] "Heightism" has been identified as a form of bias because tall people as a group have a higher socio-economic status than short people.[54] A study in 2011 "found that people who rate themselves as attractive generally have higher incomes and increased marriage prospects, and are also more likely to have attractive-looking or high-earning spouses."[55] This has given us the term "beautyism" which is defined as "biased preference ... based on their bodily physical attractiveness, whilst overlooking their skills, knowledge, and abilities."[56] At least one author has a different slant on "beautyism"; "In most cases, [beautyism] is characterized by the assumption that "attractive" people are not smart or intellectual."[57] These "-isms" illustrate the fact that if different groups in society are compared with each other, there will inevitably be socio-economic disparities.

The fact that there are socio-economic disparities does not explain what causes the disparities. Historic discrimination in the form of slavery and subsequent Jim Crow laws, as well as discrimination in employment and education, undoubtedly contributed to many of the socio-economic disparities that still exist today in the United States. Civil rights legislation in the 1950s and 1960s could not, of course, immediately change with the stroke of a pen the circumstances in which people were living. Socio-economic disparities between ethnic groups have continued for two generations since the civil rights movement.

Proponents of CRT and their accusations of "systemic racism" refer to the myriad socio-economic disparities as both <u>examples</u> of systemic racism as well as <u>causes</u> of systemic racism. The argument that "systemic racism" causes "socio-economic disparities" and that such disparities are "systemic racism" is an obvious example of a circular reasoning fallacy:[58]

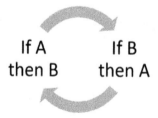

If A   If B
then B   then A

The potential for logical circularity in the analysis of racism has been recognized for at least three decades:

> If racism is defined as the behavior that results from the belief, its discovery becomes ensnared in a circularity--racism is a belief that produces behavior, which is itself racism" (citation omitted). The

existence of racism is established by racist behavior, which itself proves the existence of racism; racism, for these analysts, is a phenomenon like God: the Alpha and the Omega. This circularity stems from not grounding racism on real social relations among the races. If racism, viewed as an ideology, was seen as having a material foundation, then its examination could be associated with racial practices rather than with mere ideas, and the problem of circularity would be avoided.[59]

"Systemic racism" was frequently referred to in the past as "institutional racism." Early writings by academicians and activists in the 1970s picked up the concept that racism is the belief that one race is superior to another and has the institutional power to implement this belief in social institutions.[60]

Institutional racism relies on the active and pervasive operation of anti-black attitudes and practices. A sense of superior group position prevails: Whites are "better" than Blacks; therefore, Blacks should be subordinated to Whites. This is a racist attitude, and it permeates society, on both the individual and institutional level, covertly and overtly.[61]

The concept of "institutional racism" accordingly also constitutes a circular reasoning fallacy.

Finally, and as in the case of the dominant perspective on racism, this perspective is ensnared in circularity. Racism, which is or can be almost everything, is proven by anything done (or not done) by. Whites (Miles, 1989; 56). The analyst identifies the existence of racism because any action done by Whites is labeled as racist.[62]

The fundamental premise in CRT, according to which all socio-economic disparities between "Whites" and "Blacks" constitute systemic (institutional) racism and that racism is the usual way in which society does business"[63] has no factual basis and constitutes a fallacy due to the inherent circular reasoning in this premise.

The consequences of this fallacy are not just academic. The fallacy leads to superficially blaming "systemic racism" for socio-economic disparities and distracts from examining the underlying causes of disparities. A major consequence of the fallacy is the unavoidable conclusion that "systemic racism" is, in effect, a societal perpetual motion machine. The late law professor Derrick Bell, sometimes called the godfather of CRT,[64] stated that racism "is an integral, permanent, and indestructible component of this society."[65] This leads, in turn, to the conclusion that the only way to eliminate "systemic racism" is to trash the entire perpetual motion machine, i.e. eliminate modern American society. This goal is readily apparent in efforts throughout the country to remove symbols of the past, such as statues and names of great Americans, from public buildings. One modern writer, Ibram X. Kendi, implicitly acknowledges the circular reasoning and the self-perpetuation inherent in the concept of "systemic racism" when he calls for permanent "antiracist" discrimination:

> The only remedy to stop racist discrimination is antiracist discrimination. The only remedy to past discrimination is present discrimination. The only remedy to present discrimination is future discrimination.[66]

The flawed logic in the irrational, primary tenet of CRT has practical consequences for social policies and the law. The next, Chapter V discusses how CRT addresses socio-economic disparities with policies directed towards outward appearances, i.e. the symptoms, rather than analyzing and dealing with the underlying root causes.

2. "Interest convergence" or "material determinism"

Professor Derrick Bell developed this second pillar of Critical Race Theory in the 1970s and promulgated the "interest-convergence theory" throughout the legal community in his 1980 analysis of the *Brown v. Board of Education* 347 U.S. 483 (1954).[67] That is the landmark case that held that racial segregation inherently constitutes the unequal application of the law and overturned the "separate but equal!" doctrine established almost six decades earlier in the infamous decision in *Plessy v. Ferguson* 163 U.S. 537 (1896). Bell developed the interest-convergence theory as an overarching, general explanation for what motivates the courts and society in general to allow progress in race relations. The interest-convergence theory simply states:

> The interest of Blacks in achieving racial equality will be accommodated only when it converges with the interests of Whites.[68]

According to Bell (especially in his later writings), the *Brown v. Board of Education* decision and other court decisions and governmental policies have not been the result of any great moral insight on the part of the white Justices on the Supreme Court and other white policymakers. Bell postulates instead that progress only occurs when white interests are benefitted at least as much as minority interests. Bell and other proponents of CRT argue, for example, that the Supreme Court's decision in *Brown v. Board of Education* was supposedly based primarily on the realization that eliminating racial segregation would benefit Whites at least as much as Blacks because, at that time, the Cold War was in full swing and America was supposedly at risk of losing the debate with communism due to the stigma of segregation.

> [T]he decision in Brown to break with the Court's long-held position on these issues cannot be understood without some consideration of the decision's value to Whites, not simply those concerned about the immorality of racial inequality, but also those Whites in policymaking positions able to see the economic and political advances at home and abroad that would follow the abandonment of segregation. First, the decision helped to provide immediate credibility to America's struggle with Communist countries to win the hearts and minds of emerging third-world peoples.[69]

No explanation is provided for why the Supreme Court fails to mention this motive with a single word in the decision, although the Supreme Court invariably writes down the reasons for its judgments in the published decisions, often in excruciating detail.

American academia has produced only a few writings that have genuinely criticized Critical Race Theory and its fundamental premises, such as the "interest-convergence theory," perhaps because of fear that such criticism could adversely affect careers in academia. Professor Justin Driver, currently at Yale Law School, had the courage to challenge the interest-convergence theory in an excellent analysis published in 2011.[70]

The interest-convergence theory is a prime example of how the dialectical approach draws a simplistic line between two supposedly opposing sides, namely, between "white interests" and "black interests." Defining interests along the lines of race makes sense with regard to a system with slavery based on race: Slave owners have an economic (material) interest in maintaining slavery, while slaves have their own separate interest in having personal freedom to live their lives as they wish. The direct economic benefit obtained from forced labor in an economy based on slavery is no longer immediately apparent under segregation. Identifying specific white and black interests is a bit more difficult in a system of segregation such as that existed in the United States in the Jim Crow era. Instead, the supposed "white" interests under Jim Crow can only lie in Whites gaining opportunities for economic advancement at the expense of Blacks by depriving Blacks of those opportunities. Identifying specifically mutually opposing group interests of Blacks compared to Whites is virtually impossible in our modern, technological society with its high degree of geographic and social mobility.

The interest-convergence theory also suffers from the weakness inherent in every attempt to apply binary dialectic to analyzing society. Dividing society into just two camps of the "oppressed" and the "oppressors" or looking at society in terms of "black" (or people of color) and "white" ignores all factors which are not defined by the criterion used to draw the line between two sides. However, the development of any society, and especially our modern American society, is influenced by countless factors and interests of individuals and groups that have nothing to do with race.

Now that almost seven decades have passed since *Brown v. Board of Education* started the demise of the Jim Crow era, it is difficult to imagine what interests are specifically "white" and what interests are specifically "black," and it is even more difficult to determine how any such racial interests oppose each other. For example, both Whites and Blacks have a common interest in being safe from crime, which is why the demands to defund police departments in 2020 after the death of George Floyd are no longer in the headlines, with only the most ardent militants still calling for defunding or eliminating police departments. However, if "black" interests are the same as "white" interests, there is no longer a foundation for the interest-convergence theory. The logic is simple: If "white" and "black" interests are already the same, there are no different interests that can converge with each other.[71]

The interest-convergence theory is refuted by facts. If this doctrine were correct, i.e. if society and especially the courts only advance "black" interests if "white" interests are also advanced, how can affirmative action be explained? Although a "black" interest is perhaps identifiable because more Blacks are admitted to graduate schools or hired under affirmative action programs, there is no readily apparent "white" interest in having necessarily lower admissions and hiring. Professor Richard Delgado, perhaps the leading proponent of CRT in America today, referring to Derrick Bell's work on interest convergence, takes an extremely cynical, convoluted approach in order to identify a "white" interest in the form of restraining competition from "people of color"

> At best, then, affirmative action serves as a homeostatic device, assuring that only a small number of women and people of color are hired or promoted [...]. Not too many, for that, would be terrifying, nor too few, for that, would be destabilizing. Just the right small number, generally those of us who need it least, are moved ahead.[citation omitted] [72]

Delgado amplifies his cynicism a couple of pages later when he characterizes affirmative action as an instrument developed by the white majority intended to assuage white guilt while keeping minorities from too much advancement:

> Well, if you were a member of the majority group and invented something that cut down the competition, made you feel good and virtuous, made

minorities grateful and humble, and framed the "minority problem" in this wondrous way, I think you would be pretty pleased with yourself. [73]

At least one legal scholar Douglas Litowitz, who generally recognizes some value in CRT and has also expressed support for affirmative action, clearly acknowledges the fact that the interest-convergence theory fails when applied to affirmative action:

> [T]here is no evidence that Whites allow affirmative action because it benefits them, and in fact, the opposite is true - most Whites who endorse affirmative action (myself included) believe that it will work to their personal detriment but nevertheless feel that it is required by justice. [74]

The proponents of CRT and the interest-convergence theory try to explain all progress in race relations with the cynical concept that progress only results when white interests are benefitted. The situation for black Americans and, for that matter, all "people of color" has clearly improved since the end of World War II, but what are the "white" interests that have converged with this progress? The only apparent "white" interest lies in living in a country without race discrimination and perhaps assuaging "white guilt." The search for uniquely "white" interests that converge with "black" interests in every instance of progress in racial relations, as argued by Professor Bell, yields results that are so nebulous that the search is comparable to the stereotypical high school English teacher insisting that the students search for a story's "hidden meaning" in a homework assignment. Everyone who has graduated high school can recall how a bit of creativity makes it possible to find "hidden meaning" in everything, regardless of whether or not the original author intended the "hidden meaning."

The interest-convergence theory is just as creative in finding, however tortuously, the "hidden meaning" consisting of the majority's self-interest as the driving factor for any progress while ignoring all other factors as well as cases in which the interest-convergence theory makes no sense, no matter how much effort is devoted to searching for "white" interests. There are, in fact, many court cases involving race that do not fall within the parameters of the interest-convergence theory.[75] The "find the hidden meaning" technique employed by Bell under interest-convergence theory also has the consequence that a "white" interest can be anything. The lack of precision in the term and how it is used means that trying to delineate an interest is tantamount to trying to "nail Jello to the wall." There is accordingly no way to test the theory; a theory that cannot be falsified in a specific case under any test whatsoever is useless:

> Like many self-styled prophets, however, Professor Bell can tout his foresight, not least because he espouses a view of the world that is fundamentally incapable of being falsified by subsequent events. All judicial decisions involving race can, if subjected to sufficiently intense scrutiny, be understood to affirm the existence of the interest-convergence theory at work. [*citation omitted*] The interest-convergence theory's irrefutability, moreover, is intensified by Professor Bell's tendency to minimize and ignore data points that appear to refute or even complicate the thesis.[76]

The interest-convergence theory is fundamentally unsound because it is based on identifying distinct "black" interests and distinct "white" interests. The search for such distinct interests fails in many situations unless the contours of interests become so fuzzy as to be meaningless. The interest-convergence theory is a doctrine based on a dialectic "black" versus "white" view of the law and American society in general. The interest-convergence theory is accordingly simplistic because it ignores other factors which influence court decisions and governmental policies. The interest-convergence theory assumes that racial self-interest is determinative and that "Whites" as a group do not make decisions about race on the basis of morality or basic concepts of equal treatment under the law. The consequence is that Bell and other proponents believe that racism is a permanent feature in American society that can only be met with permanent resistance.[77] This general cynicism about an entire ethnic group expressed in the interest-convergence theory is itself racist (under the traditional definition).

3. Race as a "social construct"

As discussed above with regard to the definition of the term racism, at least this premise in Critical Race Theory is theoretically correct when stating that there is no direct biological or genetic component to race. However, due to this premise's simplicity and absoluteness, this concept fails to acknowledge the obvious fact that societies often use physical characteristics such as skin color, facial features, and other external appearances common to a large group of people as a means of defining a race and that these superficial elements are genetically determined. Terms such as black, white, yellow, red, and brown refer to genetically determined physical appearance and are often used to designate races. Proponents of CRT would otherwise not use the term "people of color" to refer to ethnic minorities. All people, of course, belong to the species *homo sapiens* and are members of the "human race." However, the term "race" in the context of CRT refers to groups of people who are perceived by society to have common physical or cultural traits.

4. "Differential racialization"

The doctrine of "differential racialization" is yet another example of the pseudo-intellectual jargon which is so typical for Critical Race Theory and Critical Theory in general. However, the doctrine is, in fact, simply another example of the dialectic approach which divides society into the oppressed and the oppressor classes along racial lines.

The doctrine of differential racialization assumes that "the dominant society "racializes different minority groups at different times, in response to shifting needs such as the labor market."[78] The word "racialization" refers to the process by which society delineates different "races" and attributes characteristics to the races;[79] i.e. racialization is how society creates a race as a "social construct." Every human society experiences changes and evolves over time, sometimes at a very slow pace, such as in the Middle Ages, and sometimes in just one generation. The delineation of races and the attributes assigned to them are accordingly not static.[80] Common examples of "differential racialization" are the ways in which Jews, the Irish, Italians, the Chinese, the Japanese, Hispanics, Blacks, and others have been viewed over time. Sometimes ethnic groups were favored because they provided labor, such as the Chinese, who were later vilified as a group under the Chinese Exclusion Act of 1882. Americans of German and Japanese ethnicity have been viewed favorably and also treated harshly in times of war, only to soon afterward be viewed favorably again.

Racialization occurs by attributing various (usually) negative stereotypes to a minority group.[81] Typical examples of generally attributed negative characteristics or stereotypes are easy to find throughout American society, especially in the past. Everyone reading this work is well aware of examples of negative attributes, so there is no need to provide examples here. Racialization might also include attributing a positive characteristic, such as when ethnic groups are viewed as being hard workers or smart or frugal (or with a negative slant, cheap). Racialization is accordingly generally harmful to the individual members of the minority group because it weakens viewing and evaluating people as individuals.

The term "needs" in the definition of "differential racialization" is extremely vague. The example of the labor market refers to an economic need, but there can be other "needs" such as a perceived need for national security in World War II when Japanese-Americans were the subject of racism. The term "needs" in the context of "differential racialization" is, in fact, so general a term that it is equivalent to the concept of "interests" in interest-convergence theory, i.e. anything that supposedly benefits the ethnic majority ethnic group.

The doctrine of "differential racialization" is, thus, a mirror image of the "interest-convergence theory." While differential racialization posits that the needs (= interests) of the majority result in harm to minorities due to racialization and related discrimination, the "interest-convergence theory" states that positive developments for minorities only occur when there is a corresponding benefit for the majority. In other words: Both good and bad treatment of minorities is dictated by the interests of the ethnic majority. In true dialectic fashion, both doctrines divide society into two sides, "Whites" as the majority ethnic group and "Blacks" and other "people of color" as the minorities who are treated poorly in the form of racialization or positively, depending on what the majority perceives as its needs/interests.

The major intellectual flaw in both the "interest-convergence theory" as well as the concept of "different racialization" lies in the fact that both concepts assume that it is possible to identify the "interests" / "needs" of the majority "white" population that are contrary to (or different from) the interests of the minority "people of color" population. Furthermore, these two doctrines hold that members of ethnic minorities cannot control their own destinies because these doctrines state that any change in an ethnic minority's situation can only occur when the change (good or bad) coincides with substantial benefits for the "white" majority. This is an extremely fatalistic view that can only promote a strong sense of victimization.

5. "Intersectionality" and "anti-essentialism"

Academia and, specifically, the social sciences deserve credit for inventing terms that sound intellectually impressive and describe readily apparent, simple things. This is especially true for the terms "intersectionality" and "anti-essentialism." "Intersectionality" recognizes that individuals can belong to various "marginalized" groups. People are, of course, multifaceted beings with countless combinations of various features. The greater the number of specific groups in which we classify people, the greater is the chance that an individual can be classified in multiple groups. If various groups, such as Blacks, gays, women, Hispanics, etc. are each subject to "marginalization," i.e. group discrimination, it is then obvious that an individual may be subject to "marginalization" in multiple respects. For example, a black person may also be a woman, perhaps even a gay woman who might even have a Hispanic name, and she might even be Muslim or Jewish.

The discussion about "intersectionality" and "anti-essentialism" arose in Critical Race Theory circles when Kimberlé Crenshaw pointed out that the feminist concerns of all women do not include specific concerns of black women, and this discussion continued for quite some time.[82] The fact that Kimberlé Crenshaw recognized that people could be classified into multiple "marginalized" groups and coined the term "intersectionality" in 1989 to describe this self-evident point can hardly be considered a great intellectual achievement.

"Anti-essentialism" is, by definition, contrary to "essentialism." "Essentialism" in the broader philosophical sense states that an object (or person) is defined by one or more properties which must absolutely exist in such an object (or person).[83] "Anti-essentialism," especially in the context of Critical Race Theory, argues that an individual is defined by multiple characteristics and is, thus, intersectional. Simply stated, "anti-essentialism" in the context of CRT is synonymous with the term "intersectionality" and, therefore, just another example of the pseudo-intellectual sophistry involved in CRT.

6. The "voice of color thesis"

Delgado/Stefancic describe the voice of color thesis as follows:

> [T]he voice-of-color thesis holds that because of their different histories and experiences with oppression, black, Indian, Asian, and Latino/ writers and thinkers may be able to communicate to their white counterparts matters that Whites are unlikely to know. Minority status, in other words, brings with it a presumed competence to speak about race and racism.[84]

The first sentence in this definition makes some general sense because an individual's personal experience or the experiences of a person's ancestors passed down in family histories may enable an individual to communicate facts and emotions which another person who does not share the same history and experiences might not know. After all, that is the whole purpose of autobiographies and biographies because they enable the reader to understand the subject's situation.

However, this does not mean that a person with minority status necessarily has the knowledge about family history or "has experiences with oppression" that yield some special insight, contrary to what the second sentence in the definition states.

The "voice of color thesis" also fails to recognize the fact that people can understand the oppression and pain suffered by other people without belonging to the victimized ethnic group. That is why people who, for example, watch a movie such as "Schindler's List" or other movies about the Holocaust are deeply moved despite not being Jewish. The miniseries "Roots" in the mid-1970s had a major impact on the entire country, although only one of the four directors was black (Gilbert Moses) while the other three directors were white (Marvin Chomsky, John Erman, David Greene).

The main effect of the "voice of color thesis" in practice is to suppress discussion. This is exemplified in a blog post published in 2014 by Reni Eddo-Lodge, a writer in the United Kingdom who has, in the meantime, published a book under the same title as the blog post *Why I am No Longer Talking to White People about Race*.[85] The "voice of color thesis" is also in play in virtually every TV news show in which a panel discusses racial issues and consists almost exclusively of Blacks and the occasional Asian or Hispanic person. Some authors take the view that "Whites" should simply shut up when race is discussed.

> Maybe we should listen — by reading what black people have written and are writing; by paying attention to what black people are saying about what helps and what doesn't. Only by shutting up for a second will we learn when we should shut up.[86]

The "voice of color thesis" attributes a presumption of competence simply on the basis of a person's race and is, thus, clearly racist under the classic definition of racism.

This thesis also begs the question of why the supposedly intellectual doctrine of Critical Race Theory uses this thesis to suppress criticism by individuals who, although having studied the material intensely, do not belong to the appropriate ethnic minority.

7. Storytelling

Stories about specific experiences of individuals can trigger strong emotional reactions. We have all felt the "Thrill of victory ... The agony of defeat"[87] when watching sports movies. We have all experienced sadness when watching tear-jerkers such as *Love Story* or tragic war movies such as *Saving Private Ryan*, regardless of whether the stories are real or fiction.

> "Everyone loves a story." The hope is that well-told stories describing the reality of black and brown lives can help readers to bridge the gap between their worlds and those of others. Engaging stories can help us understand what life is like for others and invite the reader into a new and unfamiliar world.[88]

Emotional reaction is a key factor in entertainment, and emotion can also be a major aspect of political activism. It's virtually impossible to reshape a society with a complacent, satisfied population. Given enough outrage, a revolution is possible. A dramatic story, whether true or not, can trigger riots or motivate a mob to lynch an innocent person. Emotions are inherent in every person. Of course, everyone also has the capacity for rational thought. Whether emotions and rational thought are opposites, as argued by the ancient Greek philosopher Plato and David Hume (1711–1776), and, thus, preclude each other, or whether emotions and rational thought complement each other[89] is irrelevant for the purpose of understanding Critical Race Theory. However, social analysis and developing policies cannot do without rational thought, and sometimes emotions override rational thought to the point that analysis and civil discourse are rendered impossible.

Storytelling is particularly important for CRT as an ideology. CRT is both a way of looking at society, albeit simplistic and misguided, and also a political ideology with specific goals. No political ideology can succeed by relying only on stale platitudes and tedious debate about ideological nuances. A political ideology needs activists who are willing to do what is necessary to further the ideology, including violence if necessary. Stories serve the useful purpose of whipping up emotion, regardless of whether the specific story is true, as has been readily apparent in recent years.

Chapter Summary

The foundational concepts of Critical Race Theory do not survive a focused analysis. The definition of "racism" to include the element of "power" distorts the term and leads to absurd conclusions that a "person of color" cannot be racist while all "Whites" are inherently racist because they are part of the "white power structure." The primary tenet of CRT, according to which racism is everywhere in American society, the normal way we do business in America today, has no basis in law or fact. Socio-economic disparities between different ethnic groups exist, but socio-economic disparities cannot logically constitute systemic racism since that would be circular logic and, thus, make no sense. "Interest-convergence theory" and its counterpart "differential racialization" are simplistic (not to say simple-minded) doctrines that conclude that the destiny of an ethnic minority, both good and bad, is determined by the interests of the "white" majority. This is a fatalist view which holds that members of an ethnic minority have little agency over their own future. "Race as a social construct" as well as "intersectionality" are self-evident points that do not deserve anything close to the amount of academic ink spent on them. Finally, CRT relies on the "voice of color thesis" to suppress legitimate criticism in a manner that is truly racist while at the same time emphasizing the emotionality of "storytelling."

---

[1]   Delgado/Stefancic, pg. 8.

[2]   Ibid., pg. 9.

[3]   Ibid:, pg. 9.

[4]   Ibid., pg. 10.

[5]   Crenshaw, Kimberlé, "*Demarginalizing the Intersection of Race and Sex: A Black Feminist Critique of Antidiscrimination Doctrine, Feminist Theory and Antiracist Politics*", University of Chicago Legal Forum: Vol. 1989: issue. 1, Article 8. Available at: https://chicagounbound.uchicago.edu/cgi/viewcontent.cgi?article=1052&context=uclf.

[6]   Delgado/Stefancic, pg. 8.

[7]   Ibid., pp. 44 – 54.

[8]   Ibid. pg. 49.

[9]   Frank Xu, president of the Californians for Equal Rights Foundation, quoted by CBS8 television on June 28, 2021 at https://www.cbs8.com/article/news/verify/what-is-critical-race-theory-verify/509-fb1e4db1-c3dc-4131-9e35-f7d733ae3c5a.

[10]   Elliott C. McLaughlin, "Critical race theory is a lens. Here are 11 ways looking through it might refine your understanding of history", CNN (May 27, 2021), https://www.cnn.com/2021/05/27/us/critical-race-theory-lens-history-crt/index.html.

[11]   David R. Boediger, "Historic Foundations of Race", National Museum of African American History, at https://nmaahc.si.edu/learn/talking-about-race/topics/historical-foundations-race.

[12]   See e.g., Kay S. Hymnowitz, "Uniquely Bad – But Not Uniquely American", City Journal (October 18, 2020), at https://www.city-journal.org/article/uniquely-bad-but-not-uniquely-american.

---

13   A discussion of the 95 Theses is available at https://www.theopedia.com/95-theses.

14   Available at https://www.ourdocuments.gov/doc_large_image.php?flash=false&doc=84.

15   Col. Jonathan Dahms, "Army commemorates 60th anniversary of Armed Forces Integration", published by the U.S. Army (July 24, 2008), https://www.army.mil/article/11187/army_commemorates_60th_anniversary_of_armed_forces_integration.

16   Text available at https://www.trumanlibrary.gov/library/executive-orders/9980/executive-order-9980.

17   Text available at https://tile.loc.gov/storage-services/service/ll/usrep/usrep347/usrep347483/usrep347483.pdf.

18   *Brown v. Board of Education of Topeka*, 349 U.S. 294, available at https://perma.cc/B6BV-6UGV.

19   Current text available at: https://leginfo.legislature.ca.gov/faces/codes_displaySection.xhtml?lawCode=CIV&sectionNum=51.

20   Text at: https://leg.wa.gov/CodeReviser/documents/sessionlaw/1949c183.pdf?cite=1949%20c%20183%20%C2%A7%202.

21   https://www.loc.gov/item/2008679853/.

22   Delgado/Stefancic, pg. 185.

23   Bailey Maryfield, "Implicit Racial Bias", Justice Research and Statistics Institute, December 2018, at https://www.jrsa.org/pubs/factsheets/jrsa-factsheet-implicit-racial-bias.pdf.

24   See, e.g., Devah Pager, Bruce Western, Bart Bonikowski, "Discrimination in a Low-Wage Labor Market: A Field Experiment", American Sociological Review (2009), Vol 74, pp 777 – 799), https://scholar.harvard.edu/files/bonikowski/files/pager-western-bonikowski-discrimination-in-a-low-wage-labor-market.pdf.

25   Ibid. pp. 1, 2.

26   Ibid. pg. 788.

27   Ibid. pg. 793.

28   Ibid. pg. 793.

[29] Patrick Kline, Evan Rose, Christopher Walters, "Systemic Discrimination Among Large U.S. Employers", National Bureau of Economic Research (July 2021), available at https://www.nber.org/papers/w29053.

[30] Ibid. pg. 90.

[31] Ibid. pg. 1.

[32] Ibid. pg. 1.

[33] Michael Stoll, Steven Raphael, Harry Holzer, "Why Are Black Employers More Likely than White Employers to Hire Blacks?", Institute for Research on Poverty (August 2001), https://www.irp.wisc.edu/publications/dps/pdfs/dp123601.pdf.

[34] Ibid. pp. 30, 31.

[35] Akash Peshin, "What Is The Higgs Boson? Why Is It Called The 'God Particle'?", January 6, 2022, Science ABC, https://www.scienceabc.com/nature/universe/why-is-higgs-boson-called-the-god-particle.html.

[36] Test yourself at https://implicit.harvard.edu/implicit/takeatest.html.

[37] Nicholas Kristof, "What? Me Biased?", The New York Times (October 28, 2008), https://www.nytimes.com/2008/10/30/opinion/30kristof.html.

[38] Jesse Singal, "Psychology's Favorite Tool for Measuring Racism Isn't Up to the Job" in "The Cut", at https://www.thecut.com/2017/01/psychologys-racism-measuring-tool-isnt-up-to-the-job.html.

[39] German Lopez, "For years, this popular test measured anyone's racial bias. But it might not work after all", Vox.com (March 7, 2017), https://www.vox.com/identities/2017/3/7/14637626/implicit-association-test-racism.

[40] Anthony Greenwald, Miguel Brendl, Huajian Cai, *et al.* "Best research practices for using the Implicit Association Test", Behav Res 54, pp. 1161 – 1180 (2022), available at https://doi.org/10.3758/s13428-021-01624-3.

[41] "Systemic Racism: 64 Practical Examples of the Challenges that Face Black Americans" lists and links to 64 studies, https://curiousrefuge.com/blog/systemic-racism.

[42] Ibid.

[43]   "Disparities in Wealth by Race and Ethnicity in the 2019 Survey of Consumer Finances," in FEDS Notes published by the Board of Governors of the Federal Reserve System (September 28, 2020), https://www.federalreserve.gov/econres/notes/feds-notes/disparities-in-wealth-by-race-and-ethnicity-in-the-2019-survey-of-consumer-finances-20200928.htm.

[44]   Table "Racial Demographics of Associate Degree Holders", https://educationdata.org/education-attainment-statistics.

[45]   Table "U.S. Adults over 25 with a Bachelor's Degree or Higher", https://educationdata.org/education-attainment-statistics.

[46]   Ibid.

[47]   Kristin Takata, "A legacy of systemic racism: Black students, especially boys, still being suspended at far greater rates", The San Diego Union-Tribune (February 20, 2021), https://www.recordnet.com/story/news/education/2021/02/20/a-legacy-systemic-racism-black-students-suspended-far-greater-rates-california/4524735001/.

[48]   "Expanded Homicide Table 3" published by the Criminal Justice Information Services Division of the U.S. Department of Justice, https://ucr.fbi.gov/crime-in-the-u.s/2019/crime-in-the-u.s.-2019/tables/expanded-homicide-data-table-3.xls.

[49]   "Race and Ethnicity of Violent Crime Offenders and Arrestees, 2018", Allen J. Beck, Bureau of Justice Statistics at the U.S. Department of Justice, January 2021, https://bjs.ojp.gov/content/pub/pdf/revcoa18.pdf.

[50]   Federal Bureau of Prisons, updated on March 22, 2022, https://www.bop.gov/about/statistics/statistics_inmate_race.jsp.

[51]   Statistics prepared by the Prison Policy Initiative, https://www.prisonpolicy.org/research/race_and_ethnicity/.

[52]   Chika Vera Anekwe et al., "Socioeconomics of Obesity", in National Library of Medicine (September 2021), https://www.ncbi.nlm.nih.gov/pmc/articles/PMC7484407/.

[53]   Lee Dye, "Study: 'Weightism' More Widespread Than Racism", online abc News (2008), https://abcnews.go.com/Technology/BeautySecrets/story?id=4568813&page=1.

[54]   Robin Hughes, "All Height Matters: Implicit Bias and Unearned Privileges", in the online publication "Diverse – Issues in Higher Education" (2016), https://www.diverseeducation.com/faculty-

staff/article/15099241/all-height-matters-implicit-bias-and-unearned-privileges.

55   Kimberly Chin, "Beauty & the Bills: Wealth Tied to Good Looks", published in "The Street" (March 31, 2011), https://www.thestreet.com/personal-finance/beauty-bills-wealth-tied-good-looks-12788129.

56   " 'Beautyism' in the Workplace Case Study" (2020), online in IvyPanda, https://ivypanda.com/essays/beautyism-in-the-workplace/.

57   Ryan Fisher, "Beautyism: Definition and Use", online at "business writing" (August 16, 2022), https://www.businesswritingblog.com/business_writing/2022/08/beautyism-definition-and-use.html.

58   Britannica, "circular argument" at https://www.britannica.com/topic/circular-argument.

59   Bobilla-Silva, Eduardo, "Rethinking Racism: Towards a Structural Interpretation", working paper for the Center for Research on Social Organization (October 1994) pg.19, quoting from Yehudi O. Webster, The Racialization of America, New York: St. Martin's Press (1992), pg. 84, available at https://deepblue.lib.umich.edu/bitstream/handle/2027.42/51290/526.pdf?sequence=1://deepblue.lib.umich.edu/bitstream/handle/2027.42/51290/526.pdf?sequence=1.

60   Ibid., pp. 16, 17.

61   Stokely Carmichael, Stokely and Charles Hamilton, Black Power: The Politics of Liberation in America. (1967), New York: Vintage Books, pg. 5.

62   Bobilla-Elva, ibid. footnote 59, pg. 18, citing Miles, Robert, Racism (1989), London and New York: Routledge.

63   Delgado/Stefancic, pg. 8.

64   Adam Kirsch, "The Godfather of Critical Race Theory", The Wall Street Journal (June 25, 2021), https://www.wsj.com/articles/the-godfather-of-critical-race-theory-11624627522.

65   Derrick Bell, Faces at the Bottom of the Well; The Permanence of Racism, Basic Books (at ix (1992), pg. ix, available at https://ia600203.us.archive.org/5/items/facesatbottomofw00bellrich/facesatbottomofw00bellrich.pdf.

66   Kendi, How to be an Antiracist, pg. 31.

67   Derrick Bell, "Brown v. Board of Education and the Interest-Convergence Dilemma", Harvard Law Review Vol. 93 no. 3 (Jan. 1980), pp. 518 – 533, https://harvardlawreview.org/print/no-

volume/brown-v-board-of-education-and-the-interest-convergence-dilemma/.

[68]   Ibid., pg. 523.

[69]   Ibid., pg. 524.

[70]   Justin Driver, "Rethinking the Interest-Convergence Thesis", Northwestern University Law Review, Vol 105, No. 149 – 197 (2011), https://scholarlycommons.law.northwestern.edu/cgi/viewcontent.cgi?article=1182&context=nulr.

[71]   See, Driver, ibid. pp. 165 – 171 for an analysis which thoroughly counters the concept of opposing/convergent interests in the "interest-convergence" doctrine.

[72]   Richard Delgado, "Affirmative Action as a Majoritarian Device: Or, Do You Really Want To Be a Role Model?", 89 Michigan Law Review (1991) pp. 1222 – 1231, at 1224, https://repository.law.umich.edu/cgi/viewcontent.cgi?article=2158&context=mlr.

[73]   Ibid., pg. 1225.

[74]   Douglas E. Litowitz, *Some Critical Thoughts on Critical Race Theory*, 72 Notre Dame L. Rev. pp. 503 - 529 (1997) pg. 525, available at: http://scholarship.law.nd.edu/ndlr/vol72/iss2/5.

[75]   Justin Driver, "Rethinking the Interest-Convergence Thesis" (2011), Northwestern University Law Review, Vol 105, No. 149 – 197, pp. 181 - 188, available at https://scholarlycommons.law.northwestern.edu/cgi/viewcontent.cgi?article=1182&context=nulr.

[76]   Ibid, pg. 181.

[77]   Alexis Hoag, "Derrick Bell's Interest Convergence and the Permanence of Racism: A Reflection on Resistance", Harvard Law Review Blog (August 24, 2020), available at https://blog.harvardlawreview.org/derrick-bells-interest-convergence-and-the-permanence-of-racism-a-reflection-on-resistance/.

[78]   Delgado/Stefancic, pp. 9, 10.

[79]   Merriam-Webster dictionary, "the act of giving a racial character to someone or something : the process of categorizing, marginalizing, or regarding according to race", available at https://www.merriam-webster.com/dictionary/racialization.

[80]   Erica Campbell, "Using Critical Race Theory to Measure "Racial Competency" among Social Workers§, Journal of Sociology and Social Work, (2014) Vol. 2 No. 2 pp. 73-86 at 75, http://jsswnet.com/journals/jssw/Vol_2_No_2_December_2014/5.pdf.

81   Entry in Britannica for "Basic Tenets of critical race theory" at https://www.britannica.com/topic/critical-race-theory/Basic-tenets-of-critical-race-theory.

82   See, e.g., Jane Wong, "The Anti-Essentialism v. Essentialism Debate in Feminist Legal Theory: The Debate and Beyond", William & Mary Journal of Race, Gender, and Social Justice Volume 5 (1998-1999), Issue 2, https://scholarship.law.wm.edu/cgi/viewcontent.cgi?article=1243&context=wmjowl&httpsredir=1&referer=.

83   "Essential vs. Accidental Properties" in Stanford Encyclopedia of Philosophy (2008, revised 2020), https://plato.stanford.edu/entries/essential-accidental/, which expresses the basic concept of essentialism as follows:

"P is an *essential property* of an object o just in case it is necessary that o has P, whereas P is an *accidental property* of an object o just in case o has P but it is possible that o lacks P" (Italics in original source)

84   Delgado/Stefancic, pg. 11.

85   Alice Evans, "Book Review: Why I am No Longer Talking to White People about Race", London School of Economics (2018), https://blogs.lse.ac.uk/lsereviewofbooks/2018/03/02/book-review-why-im-no-longer-talking-to-white-people-about-race-by-reni-eddo-lodge/.

86   Molly Roberts, "The best white statement to make right now may be to shut up and listen", The Washington Post (2020), https://www.washingtonpost.com/opinions/2020/06/03/best-white-statement-may-be-shut-up-listen/.

87   This phrase was popularized by the sports announcer Jim McKay (1921-2008) in the show *Wide World of Sports* on ABC.

88   Delgado/Stefancic, pg. 49.

89   Robert C. Solomon, "Emotions and rationality" at Beritannica.com, https://www.britannica.com/science/emotion/Emotions-and-rationality.

Chapter V

Critical Race Theory in Practice

One of the most common arguments raised against attempts to ban the teaching of Critical Race Theory in local schools is that CRT is not even taught in grades K-12 and that CRT is instead an advanced concept taught in law schools and other graduate schools. Although there are, in fact, no classes titled "Critical Race Theory" in grades K-12, at least at the present time, this argument is so misleading that it is tantamount to a lie.

The divisive ideology of Critical Race Theory has spread throughout the social sciences at both the graduate and undergraduate levels in both public and private universities. Training in CRT as a basis for activism and "social justice" plays an important role in college programs to obtain teaching credentials.[1] Under the Biden Administration, CRT training has found its way into the United States military, and CRT-based training is also now common in large corporations and governmental agencies. Governor Newsome of California recently signed into law Senate Bill 1495, which requires starting in 2024 that applicants, in addition to a course component on fair housing legislation, must also complete the following:

> A component on implicit bias, including education regarding the impact of implicit bias, explicit bias, and systemic bias on consumers, the historical and social impacts of those biases, and actionable steps students can take to recognize and address their **own implicit biases.**[2]
> (emphasis added)

The political left in America is increasingly forcing people to undergo CRT indoctrination and, for example, admit that they have a bias as a precondition for obtaining professional licenses.

Critical Race Theory is not just a subject for discussion in private and government agency training programs. In the meantime, CRT has been the basis for many specific policies with practical results in a broad range of areas. The development of CRT-based policies follows a fairly common pattern. **First**, a socio-economic disparity between "Whites" and other ethnic groups is identified. **Second,** the disparity is classified as an instance of racism. As discussed above, CRT considers socio-economic differences by themselves to constitute racism without considering underlying causes, which often have nothing to do with any racism on the part of the "white" majority, a governmental agency, or a company. **Third**, a policy is developed to make the disparity disappear quickly, even if the underlying causes are not addressed. In other words: Critical Race Theory treats the superficial symptom but not the cause of socio-economic disparities. This Chapter describes this three-step approach using specific examples from various fields:

1. The criminal justice system

Critical race theory has led to major changes in the American criminal justice system. Laws determine what constitutes criminal conduct. When a crime is committed, the next step normally involves the police who catch the criminal. This is followed by prosecution before the courts and punishment, often in the form of incarceration for serious offenses. CRT has affected all four levels of the criminal justice system, namely, legislation, policing, prosecution, and incarceration. The underlying reason is the belief that the entire criminal justice system disproportionately affects Blacks and is, therefore, a primary source of "systemic racism."

Legislation and law enforcement

There have been several legislative efforts in recent years in various jurisdictions to weaken or eliminate laws that are felt to disproportionately affect "people of color." A disproportionate effect on two different groups can be mitigated by either increasing compliance by the disproportionately affected group or by simply getting rid of the law or regulation that results in the disproportionate effect.

King County, WA, bicycle helmet law

King County in the state of Washington, where the city of Seattle is located, adopted an ordinance in 1993 which required all bicyclists of any age to wear helmets. The helmet law was extended to Seattle in 2003. Following the death of George Floyd at the end of May 2020, the King County Board of Health adopted Resolution 20-08 on June 18, 2020, with the following operational language (i.e., the language embodying the actual decision without the "whereas" clauses):

A. The Board declares racism a public health crisis;

B. The Board supports King County and Public Health - Seattle & King County 64 immediately in work to advance a public health approach in addressing institutional and systemic racism;

C. The Board commits to assessing, revising, and writing its guiding documents and its policies with a racial justice and equity lens, including the Board of Health Code and annual work plan; and

D. The Board members commit to ongoing work around race and equity, such as participating in racial equity training, engaging and being responsive to communities and residents impacted by racism, especially Black and Indigenous communities, as partners in identifying and implementing solutions, establishing an agreed upon understanding of racial equity principles to work towards antiracist policies and practices and to serve as 74 ambassadors of racial equity work.[3]

A report was prepared in February/March 2021, which found: "In cities around the United States, racial disparities have been identified in police stops and infractions issued to people riding bicycles, with minority individuals and communities receiving tickets at disproportionate rates.[4] This report also found that black bicyclists were 3.8 times more likely to be cited for helmet law infractions than "white" bicyclists.[5] The King County Board of Health repealed the helmet law on February 17, 2022, despite general acknowledgment that the helmet law was saving lives. One member of the board is quoted as saying:

> The question before us yesterday wasn't the efficacy of helmets," said Girmay Zahilay, a board member who is also a member of the King County Council. "The question before us was whether a helmet law that's enforced by police on balance produces results that outweigh the harm that that law creates.[6]

The language in the resolution declaring racism to be a "public health crisis," with its references to "institutional and systemic racism," is obviously based on CRT. The first step in repealing the helmet law involved finding a socio-economic disparity (3.8 times more likely to be cited). The helmet law and its enforcement were determined to be racist in the second step, and in the third step, the socio-economic disparity was instantaneously eliminated by repealing the helmet law.

The Brain Health Alliance of Washington as well as many health professionals, strongly opposed the repeal.

"Opponents of the repeal spoke about the undisputed effectiveness of bicycle helmets in preventing traumatic brain injuries and expressed fear that a repeal would lead to an uptick in injuries and deaths."[7] This begs the question of whether racial equity under CRT should be achieved by eliminating a law that clearly protects individuals, thereby likely increasing the overall instances of severe head trauma. Continued helmet law enforcement against all bicyclists would likely save the lives of individuals in all ethnic groups.

Seattle transit fare enforcement

The Pacific Northwest and especially Seattle are fruitful areas for CRT excesses. Sound Transit, one of the two major local transit companies in Seattle, issued approximately 38,000 citations and filed over 3,000 theft charges against riders who did not pay their fares. Black riders were given 46.7% of citations and constituted 56.9% of theft charges, compared to white passengers, who got 34.5% of the citations and were the subjects of 26.9% of theft charges.[8] However, Blacks make up only 7% of the King County population and 10% of the riders.[9] Shortly after the death of George Floyd, the local transit companies in Seattle changed their fare enforcement policies by eliminating uniformed fare enforcement officers and instead using "fare ambassadors" who did not impose fines and instead tried to "educate" riders about opportunities for low-income riders to pay reduced fares.

The Seattle approach to fare enforcement followed a now familiar pattern. A disparity was identified in the socio-economic data and declared to be racist. The quick fix was to eliminate fare enforcement for everyone. However, reality caught up with Seattle when fare revenue fell from approximately $ 90 million in 2019 to approximately $ 30 million in 2020 (not just due to COVID). The local transit companies accordingly reintroduced fare enforcement.[10]

Bail reform

Many jurisdictions in the United States, such as New York and Illinois, have recently introduced cashless bail. One of the main drivers in this movement involves numerous studies which have shown that higher percentages of Blacks and Hispanics are kept in pre-trial confinement than Whites. "Studies have consistently found that African American defendants receive significantly harsher bail outcomes than those imposed on White defendants."[11]

The studies have not shown that racial prejudice is the reason. However, judges have considerable discretion in setting bail and granting pre-trial release. "Most likely, the biggest culprit of racial disparities in bail determination is discretionary power; specifically, who has it and how they use it to administer bail outcomes."[12] Aspects such as perceiving an accused as "aggressive, criminal, dangerous, irresponsible, and intimately connected to drug use and trade" and prone to flight play a significant role in bail decisions, and black men may be more likely to be attributed with such characteristics.[13]

Whether or not cashless bail is a good policy is not addressed here. Many European nations look at factors when ordering pre-trial confinement such as the risk of flight, the risk of tampering with evidence and witnesses, the risk that the suspect will commit further crimes, etc. The main point for the present discussion is that a disparity was identified and then classified as an example of racism. The superficial, quick fix of eliminating cash bail and most pre-trial detention was then chosen.

Jaywalking

Statistics in New York City for 2019 show that 90% of tickets issued for jaywalking were issued to Blacks and Hispanics, although these groups make up only 55% of the city's population.[14] The New York Police Department rejects any accusation of racial bias:

> NYPD officers have discretion," said police spokesman Al Baker, a former New York Times reporter. "Officers enforce jaywalking if a specific condition exists at that moment that would require that enforcement action without consideration of race or ethnicity.[15]

In light of the small total number of 397 issued citations in 2019 and the fact that police officers issue citations in exceptional cases involving traffic disruption or danger to individuals, there is obviously no systematic effort to persecute ethnic minorities.[16] The statistics also showed that young men between 18 and 24 were most likely to be cited.[17] The statistics indicate at least a theoretical possibility that young black and Hispanic men might engage in hazardous jaywalking at a much higher rate than other people, although there are no actual data showing that this is or is not the case. However, this did not prevent Council Speaker Corey Johnson from saying:

> We know people of color are not jaywalking more than white people, so that shows a disproportionate level of policing in that community, and that's what we're gonna look at moving forward. [18]

Similar statistics exist for other major cities, such as Los Angeles, which has prompted legislators in several states to repeal or weaken laws against jaywalking.

> Preventing police from using jaywalking as a pretext to stop Black and Brown people, especially since

under-resourced neighborhoods often lack adequate crossing infrastructure.[19]

The California "Freedom to Walk Act" took effect on January 1, 2023 and prohibits police from issuing jaywalking citations unless the violation creates an immediate danger of a collision. The obvious result is that people will jaywalk more frequently, with a likely increase in pedestrian fatalities in California from an already tragic number of 6,516 in 2020.[20] Another statistic deserves mention: black pedestrians are more than twice as likely to be fatally injured in a traffic accident than white pedestrians.[21]

It is reasonable to conclude concerning jaywalking laws that Critical Race Theory has led legislative bodies to address "systemic racism" resulting from the racial disparity in jaywalking citations by effectively getting rid of citations rather than looking at potential "root causes" such as perhaps a subculture of disrespecting the law which might be more prevalent in some communities. The likely price for this CRT-based solution is an increase in the number of vehicle accidents that injure and kill pedestrians of all races.

Restraints on police tactics

A study, "Mapping fatal police violence ..." published in 2020[22], less than one month after the death of George Floyd, led to headlines such as in United Press: "Study: Black Americans 3 times more likely to be killed by police."[23] This statistic immediately spread throughout the media and contributed to the civil unrest that shook the country during the summer of 2020 and calls to defund the police. The data used in the study were clearly a reliable basis for calculating the number of fatalities among members of different races compared to the members of those races in the overall population. The data were also broken down for different metropolitan areas, and the study revealed that Blacks in Chicago have a 6.5 times higher chance of getting killed by the police. At first glance, this study appears to confirm the image propagated by many "social justice warriors" that police are racists engaged in hunting down and murdering young black men.

Police killings of *unarmed* Blacks are another area of particular concern for the proponents of Critical Race Theory. The technique of "storytelling" has become standard practice in connection with incidents in which young black men have been killed by police or someone acting under the color of law. A common phrase in journalism is, "If it bleeds, it leads." However, whether accurately reported or not, a graphic story can trigger civil unrest. Politicians, who often need to demonstrate a sense of urgency when reacting to an incident with an almost panicky, "We've got to do something!" are then easily incentivized to change laws and regulations, regardless of whether the changes actually make sense. This has been standard procedure for decades. A few cases in the last roughly ten years

Although not a shooting by a police officer, the killing of Trayvon Martin by George Zimmerman during a neighborhood watch patrol in Florida in 2012 moved the nation; President Obama commented at the time, "If I had a son, he'd look like Trayvon."[24] George Zimmerman was eventually acquitted because the jury obviously agreed with Zimmerman's defense that he had fired in self-defense after Trayvon Martin had confronted him, knocked him to the ground, jumped on top of Zimmerman, and started banging Zimmerman's head on the cement sidewalk.[25] However, the emotional storytelling in the mainstream media about an innocent young man who was supposedly shot just for being black while walking home after buying a package of Skittles led to the founding of the organization Black Lives Matter after George Zimmerman was acquitted.[26]

The shooting of Michael Brown in Ferguson, Missouri, in 2014 was the next extremely controversial killing of an unarmed young black man. The mainstream media again jumped at the opportunity for more storytelling about a police officer shooting an innocent young man who was supposedly surrendering and yelling, "Hands up - Don't shoot." This became the battle cry for the political left and is still popular today. After a long period of riots and demonstrations across the country, the investigation by both the state and federal governments found that Officer Darren Wilson had discharged his weapon when Michael Brown, weighing close to three hundred pounds, charged Wilson and refused to stop even while Wilson was firing. Despite an intense investigation and early prejudicial comments by countless politicians, especially in the Obama Administration, Wilson was not charged with any crime or violation of civil rights because he had fired in self-defense.[27]

Politicians and activists milked the story of the "gentle giant" Michael Brown to create a completely unjustified level of outrage that led to widespread rioting. The facts are described in detail in the 86-page report of March 4, 2015, by the U.S. Department of Justice on the results of its investigation. [28] Contrary to the "Hands up - Don't shoot" legend, this investigation showed that Michael Brown's death was the consequence of a chain of foolish decisions on his part.

a. **Brown decided** to shoplift a box of cigarillos in a liquor store with video camera monitors. Brown committed the crime of theft. Didn't he realize that he was being filmed?

b. When a store employee confronted Brown as he and his friend Dorian Johnson were leaving, **Brown decided** to strong-arm the employee, turning the theft into a robbery. This was recorded on the store's video.

c. Johnson and **Brown decided** then to stroll down the middle of a street on the way back home. Did they think the store would not call the police? Did Brown and Johnson think they would be inconspicuous walking down the middle of the street?

d. Officer Wilson encountered Brown and Johnson while they were walking down the middle of the street. Wilson had already received a description of the two men who had stolen the cigarillos, which clearly matched Brown and Johnson. Wilson drove a bit in front of Brown and Johnson and then backed up and stopped his police SUV in front of Brown and Johnson. Then **Brown decided** to assault Wilson, punching him in the head and breaking a facial bone. Wilson withdrew his pistol from the holster, and **Brown decided** to grab the weapon. Two shots were discharged, one of which hit Brown in the hand. Starting a fight with an armed policeman after being stopped for a crime is completely foolish and invariably has a bad end.

e. Brown ran roughly 180 feet away from the SUV. Then **Brown decided** to turn and charge Officer Wilson, who started firing to defend himself. Even after being hit, **Brown decided** to keep charging a police officer in the face of pistol fire, nothing less than suicidal stupidity. Brown was finally dropped about 22 feet from Wilson when a bullet hit Brown in the head, killing him.

The only reasonable explanation for this string of bad decisions is that Michael Brown was an extremely big (almost 300 pounds) young man who felt he could do what he wanted without fear of serious consequences. Brown seems to have been enamored of the "gangsta" culture, failing to realize that there is a big difference between reality and what is portrayed in rap song lyrics. The Trayvon Martin and Michael Brown cases and the Eric Garner case discussed below also show that whether or not the deceased person is armed does not say much about whether or not killing is justified under the law.

These emotionally laden stories and many others, however, show that statistics about racial disparities in law enforcement and elsewhere have little informative value until they are viewed in context with factors other than racial prejudice that might influence the statistics. As is often the case with such studies and the resulting superficial articles in the media, the 2020 "Mapping fatal police violence ..." study did not look beyond the pure data and consider potential causes for the racial disparities in fatalities. Police shootings are a direct consequence of police encounters with individuals. Those encounters can range from giving traffic citations or being called to a domestic dispute to arresting an individual for homicide or some other violent crime. Although a violent confrontation can happen in any police contact, even a minor traffic violation, it is likely that there is at least a certain correlation between encounters related to violent crimes and the frequency of police using violence to subdue an individual. Therefore, if an ethnic group has a higher rate of arrests for violent crime, a higher rate of police having to use violence up to and including deadly force is to be expected.

The FBI maintains statistics about crime in the USA and ethnicity in the FBI's "Table 43"; the most recent version is for the year 2019.[29] This table reflects the data for 10,831 police agencies covering about 230 million people out of a total population of approximately 330 million people. There are approximately 18,000 federal, state, county, and local police agencies in the country.[30] The 2019 data accordingly cover roughly two-thirds of both law enforcement agencies and the population. Table 43 lists total arrests according to various offenses and ethnic groups. The defined ethnic groups in Table 43 are "White," "Black or African American," "American Indian or Alaska Native," "Asian" and "Native Hawaiian or Other Pacific Islander." No separate data are shown in Table 43 for "Hispanics," although a note at the end of the table states, "Of arrestees for whom ethnicity was reported, 19.1 percent were Hispanic or Latino."

According to an analysis published in 2021 on the basis of the numbers for 2018,[31] "Whites" make up 60.4% of the population in the USA, but only 45.0% of people arrested for "Nonfatal violent crimes" (i.e. rape, robbery, aggravated assault, and other assault, excluding murder and other non-negligent homicide). The corresponding percentages for "Black" are 12.5% of the total population and 33.0% of people arrested for "Nonfatal violent crimes," and the percentages for "Hispanic" are 18.3% of the total population and 17.6 % of the people arrested for "Nonfatal violent crimes."

The statistics in Table 43 2019 for "Murder and nonnegligent [*sic*] manslaughter" show that out of a total of 7,964 cases in 2019, 4078 arrestees (51.2%) were "Black or African American." The data show an even greater disproportionate number of Blacks arrested for robbery (52.7%), while Blacks accounted for 41.8% of arrests for "Weapons, carrying, possessing, etc." compared to 12.5% of Blacks in the total population. The data accordingly clearly show that Blacks have an arrest rate for these very serious, violent crimes of roughly three to four times the percentage of Blacks in the population. This relatively simple calculation shows that the outrage expressed in the headline about Blacks being three times more likely to be killed by police than Whites is completely unjustified. Factor "three" is a correct statistic, but it says nothing about "systemic racism" because this factor readily correlates to the statistics on crime rates.

Chokeholds are extremely effective for restraining a person who is resisting arrest, as this author can personally confirm after having learned how to apply chokeholds both with arms and a billy club in the U.S. Army in 1971 at Military Police school in Fort Gordon, Georgia. However, countless police agencies at the federal, state, and local levels have been banned from using chokeholds, especially after Eric Garner was arrested in New York City on July 17, 2014. The Eric Garner story was not accurately reported in the mainstream media and is instead an excellent example of the CRT technique of "storytelling" and how effective that technique is.

The arresting Officer Pantaleo was accused of having applied a chokehold which led to Eric Garner's death, despite the photographic evidence showing that Pantaleo did not apply a chokehold and instead used a so-called "seatbelt takedown." The arrest was recorded on video.

(Source: New York Daily News via Getty Images)

After Eric Garner refused to cooperate while being arrested for a misdemeanor of allegedly selling loose cigarettes, a practice the NYPD was tasked to stop because it reduces tax revenue for the city, the arresting Officer Pantaleo restrained Eric Garner from behind by placing his right arm under Eric Garner's right arm and wrapping his left arm around Eric Garner's neck and chin. The officer's left hand is not interlocked with the right hand. This "seatbelt takedown" was a permissible restraining move. Eric Garner continued to resist, resulting in a struggle of about 15 seconds before he was restrained. Garner can be heard on the video saying, "I can't breathe," which immediately became a popular slogan. The mere fact that Garner could say these words was proof that a chokehold did not cut off his ability to breathe at that moment; if the flow of air had been interrupted, he could not have said anything.

Garner died as a result of the incident, and there was great political pressure to prosecute Officer Pantaleo. The case dragged on before state, city, and federal authorities until 2019. The grand jury investigating the case, as well as the federal authorities, did not bring charges against Officer Pantaleo. U.S. Attorney Richard Donoghue, entrusted with the case, is quoted in 2019, "There is nothing in the video to suggest that Officer Pantaleo intended or attempted to place Mr. Garner in a chokehold."

The autopsy showed that Eric Garner died from an asthma attack and cardiac arrest and not from being choked. CBS News reported that during a disciplinary hearing for Officer Pantaleo in 2019, the medical examiner Dr. Floriana Persechino testified that what she called a chokehold triggered "a lethal sequence of events," and she is reported as saying that even a bear hug could have hastened his death given Garner's fragile health." Persechino testified before the grand jury investigating Garner's death that he weighed 395 pounds at the time of his July 2014 death. He suffered from asthma, diabetes and had a heart nearly double the size of a person in good health."[32] A medical doctor who reviewed the public evidence, i.e. the news reports and the video, summarized the cause of death as follows:

> A normal and healthy male would have been transiently distressed by the actions of the arresting officers. Mr. Garner had no margin of safety [due to morbid obesity, and other health conditions], no reserve at all, and was precariously unstable even before he was accosted. The actions of the arresting officers, undoubtedly used many times before without significant ill effect, combined with Garner's pathophysiology to rapidly produce hypoxia, very likely aggravated by carbon dioxide retention and narcosis, which suppresses the normal reflex to breathe. This was rapidly followed by cardiac arrhythmia and death.[33]
> (Brackets added)

Eric Garner probably said, "I can't breathe" because he was suffering from hypoxia (low level of oxygen in body tissues) and presumably hypoxemia (low level of oxygen in the blood), both of which frequently occur at the same time and can lead to difficulty in breathing and shortness of breath.[34] Officer Pantaleo was eventually fired by the NYPD, a foregone result in light of the political atmosphere at the time, especially in New York City under Mayor Bill de Blasio.[35]

The appeal to emotion embodied in the CRT tool of storytelling, as seen in the activist left's exploitation of tragic deaths, and the superficial approach of resolving a statistical disparity by simply eliminating the basis for the statistic have been used to justify banning various, effective police tactics in recent years. Chicago prohibited foot chases in the case of minor offenses in June 2022 after two foot chases in the spring of 2021 resulted in police shooting and killing a 13-year-old boy Adam Toledo and 22-year-old Anthony Alvarez. The police officers involved in the shootings were not charged in both cases because Toledo and Alvarez were armed.[36] The restriction on foot chases was the consequence of a longer discussion in Chicago after the *Chicago Tribune* conducted an analysis in 2016, which showed that more than one-third of the 235 examined police confrontations between 2010 and 2016 that ended with someone being wounded or killed involved foot pursuits and that about half of the foot pursuits started with police stopping or questioning a person with regard to relatively minor offenses such as curfew violations, being drunk in public, theft, creating a disturbance etc.[37] A racial component apparently played a role in adopting the policy. The Chicago police department and many other departments were the subject of civil rights investigations during the Obama Administration, and according to the *Chicago Tribune*:

> Federal investigators will be particularly interested in how police shootings have disproportionately affected minorities, according to the experts. While African-Americans made up 80 percent of all those shot by police in the six-year span examined by the Tribune, an even higher number of those shot during foot chases — 94 percent — were black, the Tribune found.[38]

Baltimore, Maryland, limited police pursuits in its Policy 1505, published on February 9, 2021.[39] Portland, Oregon, adopted a policy restricting foot pursuits even with regard to armed suspects that took effect at the start of 2022. According to the policy:

3.1   [Police officers] shall not engage in or continue foot pursuits in the following circumstances:

3.1.1. Armed suspects unless, in extreme circumstances, no other alternative strategy is feasible and a delay in the apprehension of the suspect would present a threat of death or serious physical injury to others; ...[40]

Car chases have been banned in many jurisdictions, where the bans are often justified by referring to the risk for uninvolved third parties.[41] Washington State adopted a particularly restrictive statute in 2021 in the form of RCW (Revised Code of Washington) 10.116.060[42] , which reads:

(1) A peace officer may not engage in a vehicular pursuit, unless:

(a)(i) There is probable cause to believe that a person in the vehicle has committed or is committing a violent offense or sex offense as defined in RCW 9.94A.030, or an escape under chapter 9A.76 RCW; or

(ii) There is reasonable suspicion a person in the vehicle has committed or is committing a driving under the influence offense under RCW 46.61.502;

(b) The pursuit is necessary for the purpose of identifying or apprehending the person;

(c) The person poses an imminent threat to the safety of others and the safety risks of failing to apprehend or identify the person are considered to be greater than the safety risks of the vehicular pursuit under the circumstances; and

(d)(i) Except as provided in (d)(ii) of this subsection, the officer has received authorization to engage in the pursuit from a supervising officer and there is supervisory control of the pursuit. The officer in consultation with the supervising officer must consider alternatives to the vehicular pursuit. The supervisor must consider the justification for the vehicular pursuit and other safety considerations, including but not limited to speed, weather, traffic, road conditions, and the known presence of minors in the vehicle, and the vehicular pursuit must be terminated if any of the requirements of this subsection are not met;

This policy has had the obvious effect that an increasing number of suspects simply ignore the police lights and sirens. One reported case involved an attempt by a state trooper to pull over a white BMW in April 2022 because the car had a stolen license plate. The car sped off at a high rate of speed, and the trooper did not try to chase the car.[43] After the new law went into effect at the start of 2022, there was a major increase by May 2022 to more than 900 incidents of drivers ignoring police attempting to pull them over with lights and sirens.[44]

The basic approach under Critical Race Theory for remedying supposed "systemic racism" in the form of racial disparities in the criminal justice system is, in effect, to treat only the symptom. Instead of dealing with the complex socio-economic and cultural causes of high crime rates among black Americans, the solution under Critical Race Theory is simply to reduce the number of arrests by making it increasingly difficult for police to apprehend criminals in general.

The search for socio-economic disparities of any kind has, in fact, become an absurd parlor game. Perhaps nothing epitomizes this more than Assembly Bill 742, introduced by Democratic Assemblymen Corey Jackson and Ash Kalra in

California on February 13, 2023, to prohibit the use of police dogs for making arrests and crowd control as well as prohibiting all biting, for example, the arm of a suspect holding a firearm.[45] Aside from referring to the obvious risk of injury to a suspect when a dog is used, AB 742 expressly refers in section 1 (c) to the statistical disparity between races when comparing incidents of the use of canine force to the overall population:

> The use of police canines mirrors other biases in the use of force by police. Per the Department of Justice Use of Force data from 2016 to 2019, inclusive, Black people are 3.5 times more likely than any other group to be subjected to the use of force due to police canine use, with Hispanic people being the second most likely compared to cases involving White people at six per one million people.

This argument completely ignores the fact that Blacks, for example, have disproportionately higher crime rates than Whites and Asians, especially in the area of violent crime and weapons offenses.[46] The fact that police dogs are more likely to be used against persons suspected of violent crimes and weapons offenses reasonably explains the statistical disparity. Therefore, the long-term solution to the disproportionate use of police dogs is to eliminate the higher rate of violent crime, a process that is much more difficult and time-consuming than the superficial approach of generally prohibiting the use of police dogs for arrests, crowd control, etc.

Prosecution

District attorneys have broad "prosecutorial discretion" and are, accordingly, the most powerful component in the criminal justice system. United States Attorney General

Robert Jackson described the power of the prosecutor in a speech more than 82 years ago as follows:

The prosecutor has more control over life, liberty, and reputation than any other person in America. His discretion is tremendous. He can have citizens investigated, and if he is that kind of person, he can have this done to the tune of public statements and veiled or unveiled intimations. Or the prosecutor may choose a more subtle course and simply have a citizen's friends interviewed. The prosecutor can order arrests, present cases to the grand jury in secret session, and on the basis of his one-sided presentation of the facts, can cause the citizen to be indicted and held for trial. He may dismiss the case before trial, in which case the defense never has a chance to be heard. Or he may go on with a public trial. If he obtains a conviction, the prosecutor can still make recommendations as to the sentence, as to whether the prisoner should get probation or a suspended sentence, and after he is put away, as to whether he is a fit subject for parole. While the prosecutor, at his best, is one of the most beneficent forces in our society, when he acts from malice or other base motives, he is one of the worst.[47]

Any political movement looking to reduce incarceration rates for specific ethnic groups would accordingly do well to get prosecutors appointed and elected who will use the power of the office for this purpose. This is the concept behind the "Progressive Prosecution Movement,"[48] which gained substantial impetus from a speech by then former President Obama in September 2018.

If you are really concerned about how the criminal justice system treats African-Americans, the best way to protest is to vote - not just for Senators and

Representatives, but for mayors and sheriffs and state legislators. Do what they just did in Philadelphia and Boston, and elect state's attorneys and district attorneys who are looking at issues in a new light, ...[49]

President Obama was referring to Rachael Rollins, who had just won the Democratic primary for the office of District Attorney in Suffolk County (Boston), Massachusetts, and Larry Krasner, who was elected as District Attorney in Philadelphia in 2017 and assumed office on January 1, 2018. They are among around 30 progressive prosecutors, such as Kim Foxx in Chicago and George Gascón in Los Angeles, who have taken office since 2016. That group also included Chesa Boudin, whose views were so "progressive" that even the voters in San Francisco felt it necessary to remove him from office in a recall election in 2022 with a vote of 55% to 45%.[50]

Critical Race Theory is the ideological basis for progressive prosecutors when performing or refusing to perform the duties of their office in order to achieve their overarching goal of eliminating "mass incarceration" and reducing racial disparities in the criminal justice system.[51] This is readily apparent upon examination of their policies. George Gascón, for example, immediately implemented a number of policies directed toward this goal. His campaign website published a list of these policies on the day he took office: "[The Los Angeles District Attorney, "LADA"] will no longer request cash bail for any misdemeanor, non-serious or non-violent felony offense. ... Experts estimate that hundreds of individuals behind bars today will be eligible to be freed tomorrow under this new pretrial release policy." "In any case charged from this day forward, LADA will not seek the death penalty." He refused to support the Three Strikes law. He directed that the *habeas corpus* litigation unit in the LADA would use the maximum leeway available under the law "[i]n every case, where any injustice is uncovered, including racial injustice, whether or not it is of a constitutional magnitude." "LADA will immediately end the practice of transferring kids to adult court"; in other words, juvenile offenders, including killers, could no longer be tried as adults. "LADA will stop charging a number of low-level offenses associated with poverty, addiction, mental illness ...."[52]

Big-money donors to the Democratic Party have recognized the importance of financing progressive candidates for district attorneys who implement soft-on-crime policies. George Soros has spent more than $29 million, mostly through political action committees ("PACs"), on campaigns to elect progressive prosecutors in recent years and has succeeded in at least 20 jurisdictions, including major cities.[53] George Gascón in Los Angeles benefitted from almost $ 3 million. Kim Garner, originally elected in St. Louis with a record of incompetence, received $116,000 from Soros for her 2020 reelection campaign and by 2021 enabled St Louis to get the prize as "one of the deadliest cities in the world."[54] Soros helped Kim Foxx get elected in Cook County, Illinois, with $2 million. Alvin Bragg won his election as the District Attorney in Manhattan with approximately $1.1 million in assistance from George Soros, and Larry Krasner in Philadelphia has received more than $2 million in support from Soros.

Progressive prosecutors, however, are not all-powerful. State authorities can rein in some of the excesses. Governor Ron DeSantis in Florida removed the Hillsborough County district attorney in August 2022 for refusing to enforce Florida law related to abortion and establishing a policy of not prosecuting cases involving trespassing at a business location, disorderly conduct, disorderly intoxication, prosecution and crimes where the initial encounter between law enforcement and the defendant resulted from a bicycle or pedestrian violation.[55] However, removal from office is extremely rare in states where the governor has such power. Recall elections are also very difficult in states where that option is available. A costly effort to remove George Gascón fell short of the necessary number of signatures on the recall petition. The recall of Chesa Boudin succeeded only because his incompetence led 55% of the participating voters to throw him out of office.

The policies implemented by progressive prosecutors are intended to reduce racial disparities in the criminal justice system simply by not allowing the system to function in many situations. This approach treats the symptoms of the social disease "crime," namely, prosecution and punishment, by allowing certain levels of especially petty crime to flourish. Other tools, such as diversion programs, are also used, but they do little to reduce the underlying socio-economic and especially cultural factors that contribute to higher crime rates in many minority communities.

Incarceration

Proponents of Critical Race Theory reflexively point to different incarceration rates among ethnic groups as an example of systemic/institutional racism.[56] There are many organizations devoted to so-called criminal justice reform, such as The Sentencing Project. This organization describes its mission as follows:

> The Sentencing Project advocates for effective and humane responses to crime that minimize imprisonment and criminalization of youth and adults by promoting racial, ethnic, economic, and gender justice.

This organization has compiled data from the individual states, which show that, on average, Blacks are incarcerated at the state (not federal) level at a rate 4.8 times higher than

Whites when compared to the total population of each group.[57] The much higher crime rate among "Blacks" compared to "Whites," especially in the area of violent crimes, including murder and non-negligent manslaughter, provides a reasonable explanation for this socio-economic disparity. Especially in light of the argument that historical slavery and Jim Crow laws have supposedly contributed to such disparities, the expectation would be that the disparities in incarceration rates would be especially large in the Deep South. However, according to The Sentencing Project, the states with the greatest incarceration rates of Blacks compared to Whites, i.e. the number of black prisoners for each white prisoner, are (in descending order):[58]

New Jersey	12.5
Vermont	12.3
Wisconsin	11.9
Minnesota	9.9
Connecticut	9.4
Iowa	9.3
California	9.2

The incarceration rates in states in the Deep South are much lower; in fact, they are among the lowest in the country, as shown in the following list (in ascending order):[59]

Mississippi	2.6
Alabama	2.8
Georgia	2.8
Tennessee	3.4
Arkansas	3.5
Texas	3.5

Louisiana	3.8
South Carolina	3.8
North Caroline	3.9
Florida	4.1

The only states outside the Deep South with comparably low incarceration rates for Blacks compared to Whites are Hawaii (2.4), Kentucky (2.9), and Missouri (3.6).[60] The impact of historical slavery and Jim Crow is apparently negligible today, at least with regard to incarceration rates.

The easiest way to remedy the supposed structural racism of disparate incarceration rates would be to abolish prisons; incarceration rates would not even exist if there were no incarceration. The prison abolitionist movement has been around at least since Angela Davis and her activism in the late 1960s, especially her efforts to gain the release of the prisoner George Jackson and two other "Soledad Brothers" who were accused of murdering a guard. Those efforts ended with Jonathan Jackson, George's 17-year-old younger brother, and three San Quentin convicts in a courtroom in Marin County, California, kidnapping a judge and two other hostages in an attempt to extort freedom for George Jackson. Jonathan Jackson and two of the convicts were killed in the subsequent shootout, and the judge was murdered when one of the kidnappers fired a shotgun that was taped below the judge's chin.[61] Angela Davis was linked to the kidnapping because the firearms used in the kidnapping were registered in her name. She was tried for murder in 1972 for having allegedly conspired with Jonathan Jackson, but the only tangible evidence was the fact that she owned the firearms, and she stated that she had no idea of what Jonathan was planning. An all-white jury found her innocent (another example of white supremacy?).[62]

The prison abolition movement has continued since then but remained an isolated movement on the left that was not taken seriously. This changed after the death of George Floyd in May 2020. According to one of the current leaders in the prison abolition movement Keeranga-Yahmahita Taylor writing one year later, "In the past year or two, the proposition of defunding or abolishing police and prisons has travelled from incarcerated-activist networks into mainstream conversations."[63]

The federal government and individual states will certainly not completely abolish prisons and incarceration in the coming decades or probably ever (barring advancements in technology contemplated only in science fiction). However, many jurisdictions are adopting policies to reduce prison populations, especially for the purpose of reducing racial disparities. The Brennan Center for Justice at New York University School of Law, named after Supreme Court Justice William J. Brennan, published a paper in 2015, "Reducing Racial and Ethnic Disparities in Jails – Recommendation for Local Practice"[64] which discussed specific policies that in the meantime, sound tame compared to recent legislation in some states. For example, the paper proposes to "reduce reliance on pretrial detention" by using "assessment instruments" for measuring the risk that a suspect will commit more offenses if released from pretrial detention and strengthening pretrial services programs such as employment services and drug treatment and "diversion programs" as a substitute for pretrial confinement.

In the meantime, New York State and Illinois have chosen policies that are much easier to realize than applying assessment instruments and setting up pretrial services. These two states have implemented cashless bail to virtually eliminate pretrial confinement altogether. This may help reduce the racial disparity in incarceration rates, but increasing crime rates in the last few years, especially in cities such as New York and Chicago, indicate that there is a trade-off between reducing pretrial detention and the overall level of crime.

The intuitive perception is that crime rates will go down if the risk of arrest and imprisonment goes up. Whether or not this perception is accurate and whether changes in the economy in the same time period were more responsible for the decrease in crime was examined after the remarkable downturn in crime in New York City during the 1990s in a 2002 study, "Carrots, Sticks and Broken Windows" which finds after a comprehensive analysis of the data:

> Misdemeanor arrests have a significant negative impact on robbery and motor vehicle theft. This indicates that, holding constant their own arrests, the size of the police force and prison population, the growth rates in robberies and motor vehicle thefts decline as the growth rate of misdemeanor arrests increases. This result provides support for the broken windows hypothesis in case of these two crimes.[65]

This study concludes:

> While both economic and deterrence variables are important in explaining the decline in crime in New York City, the contribution of deterrence measures is larger than those of economic variables.[66]

The typical approach under Critical Race Theory with regard to the criminal justice system is superficial and does nothing to decrease crime and improve public safety, be it in society in general or predominantly ethnic minority neighborhoods. Statistical disparities between Blacks and "people of color" on the one hand and "Whites" are identified. These disparities are not the result of racism in the traditional definition of the term because no racial prejudice is apparent. Even in the George Floyd case, the prosecution never alleged that the police officers had been motivated by racial prejudice.[67] The most current, well-known case at the time of this writing involves five Memphis police officers charged with murdering Tyre Nichols by beating him to death in January 2023, but it seems that racial bias also played no role in that case because all the officers, as well as the victim, are African-Americans.[68]

Instead of addressing the underlying socio-economic and cultural reasons for statistical disparities, the CRT approach is directed towards changing primarily the statistical disparities. Proponents of Critical Race Theory focus on treating the symptom but not the underlying societal "illness." The "defund the police" movement is a typical example. An IPSOS poll taken in 2021, less than one year after the death of George Floyd, found that 41% of Blacks supported the "defund the police" movement while 52% opposed the movement (the remaining 7% did not respond).[69] If police departments were defunded to the point they could no longer effectively enforce the law, the statistical disparities in law enforcement would decrease, and if theoretically all law enforcement were eliminated, the statistical disparities would be completely eliminated simply because there would be no more law enforcement. Of course, the consequences for personal safety from a collapse of law enforcement and, in general, for society, especially in urban areas, would resemble the movie *The Purge*.

2. Education

The American education system produces a gigantic volume of data. Every student is measured throughout the student's education with regard to attendance, discipline, grades, assessment tests, graduation, advancement to college, etc. The data can be analyzed in an almost infinite number of variations by comparing the data with other information such as family income, family status (married, divorced parents, no father figure in the household, etc.), siblings, gender, geographic location, parents' education, and obesity. The data analyses show the disparities in academic performance that most readers would anticipate when considering these factors (with one exception).

- "Low family income is associated with poor academic achievement among children."[70]

- "[H]aving the benefit of two, stably married parents in their corner seems to give students an extra boost when it comes to flourishing in 21st-century schools."[71]

- "Older sibling academic engagement was the sibling relationship factor most strongly associated with younger siblings' academic outcomes, and additional factors that had a significant influence on younger siblings' academic outcomes included parent expectations of achievement and differentiation. Moreover, this influence was most consistent when the older sibling is a high achiever."[72]

- "A female advantage in school marks is a common finding in education research, and it extends to most course subjects (e.g., language, math, science), unlike what is found on achievement tests."[73]

- With regard to geographic location (urban, suburban, rural), a study published in 1998, which appears to be the most recent large study focused on this aspect, had a somewhat counterintuitive result (the one exception): "The findings of this study can be succinctly summarized as follows: the students from rural schools performed as well as their peers in metropolitan areas in the four areas of school learning: reading, math, science, and social studies. The results from this study agree with the findings of some previous studies, which found no rural/suburban/urban differences (*citation omitted*)."[74]

- "In most studies, parental education has been identified as the single strongest correlate of children's success in school, the number of years they attend school, and their success later in life."[75]

- "In recent years [up to 2012], an uneven yet growing body of research has suggested that obesity is associated with poorer academic performance beginning as early as kindergarten. Studies have variously found that obese students -- and especially girls -- tend to have lower test scores than their slimmer peers, are more likely to be held back a grade, and are less likely to go on to college....
  What's more, this pattern held even after the researchers took into account extenuating factors that can influence both body size and test scores, such as family income, race, the mother's education level and job status, and both parents' expectations for the child's performance in school."[76]

There are, of course, also the factors of race and ethnicity, with clear disparities in academic performance between ethnic groups. The "Black-White" and "Hispanic-White" achievement gaps have been recognized for decades. "The achievement gap between white students and black students has barely narrowed over the last 50 years, despite nearly a half century of supposed progress in race relations and an increased emphasis on closing such academic disparities between groups of students."[77]

Academic achievement depends on all factors discussed here and certainly many others in differing degrees. In addition to relatively tangible factors such as family income and parents' education, culture certainly plays a significant role. Not all subcultures in the United States place the same value on academic achievement. Parental expectations and encouragement, however, are extremely important factors for the education of their children and can overcome negative factors such as poverty. Dr. Ben Carson, the renowned neurosurgeon and Secretary of Housing and Urban Development during the Trump administration, is today perhaps the leading example of a young man who overcame adversity to achieve academic success, especially due to the support from his mother and despite the fact that academic performance was perhaps not so highly respected in his neighborhood.

There have been countless studies about the "Black-White" achievement gap as well as the "Hispanic-White" gap, and these studies invariably find that the achievement gaps are caused by many factors. Socio-economic status (sometimes called "SES"), parental education, family structure as well as whether or not a student is a native speaker of English are among the major factors identified for predicting academic achievement.[78] Suggestions for how to close the achievement gaps are just as varied as the factors. A 2019 paper published by Istation, an education support organization, specified eight ways "to effectively bridge the achievement differences."[79] These eight ways are intended to offset the effects of underlying problems affecting student achievement and involve both additional resources as well as an academic discipline. Furthermore, these measures can only show success over time.

- Evidence-based instruction, i.e. using assessment tools to design targeted intervention for struggling students;

- Rigorous curriculum: "Ample evidence shows that almost all students can achieve at high levels if they are taught at high levels."[80]

- Increased instructional time for struggling students tailored to their individual needs (e.g. extra time for tutoring and homework groups after regular school hours;

- Supplemental instruction to fill in any learning gaps the student might already have;

- Progress monitoring consisting of frequent assessments to identify struggling students quickly and pinpoint where they are having problems;

- Motivation and engagement, especially if the student's family does not show sufficient appreciation of learning;

- Increased resources for professional development so that teachers and other staff can identify and help struggling students early;

- Improving the connection between school and the students' families with more communication about each student's progress.

The term "equity" is extremely popular in education today and is frequently misunderstood. The basic meaning of the term is "fairness," i.e. all students have the same chances in school (equal opportunity). However, when used in the context of schools, "equity" has come to mean equal outcomes rather than equal opportunity. The above-listed measures are examples of steps that can be taken to improve the academic performance of all students. Especially when applied in the first years of school, these measures can help disadvantaged students overcome problems they might have outside school.

Critical Race Theory is not so concerned with identifying and dealing with underlying causes of socio-economic disparities since the disparity itself, according to CRT, constitutes racism. Instead, Critical Race Theory seeks to directly deal with statistical disparities in the fastest possible manner; i.e. CRT treats the symptom and not the underlying causes of the disparities. This involves in the field of education eliminating or lowering standards in the name of "diversity, equity, and inclusion" ("DEI").

Academic standards

The circular logic of Critical Race Theory, according to which disparities in socio-economic statistics themselves constitute racism, necessarily leads to the conclusion that the way to eliminate or reduce racism is to simply eliminate or reduce the statistical disparities. One way to accomplish this is to eliminate the entire set of statistics, such as what is currently happening with standardized testing. Another way to at least reduce statistical disparities is to lower academic standards. After all, that is a lot easier than putting in the hard work to raise the academic performance of children who do not (yet) meet high standards. There are countless examples of "dumbing down" education towards the lowest common denominator. Here are just a few:

The School Diversity Advisory Group recommended in 2019 that New York City phase out the "Gifted and Talented" program, which at the time accepted 2,500 students on the basis of rigorous testing, with 75% of the students being white or Asian, although those ethnic groups make up only 30% of the city's population. Mayor De Blasio decided to follow the recommendation, but he had to leave the actual implementation to his successor Mayor Eric Adams.[81] Mayor Adams did not get rid of the Gifted and Talented program. However, he "expanded" the program by eliminating the tough entrance testing and instead using an inequitable procedure (in the sense of equal treatment under the law and not in the CRT sense) to pick the students.[82]

Advanced Placement ("AP") courses have given good students the opportunity to gain recognition and high-quality instruction for many years. These courses are a key aspect of getting into high-ranked universities and winning scholarships. As is so often the case in education, Asians and Whites are disproportionately represented in AP courses compared to the general student population. Instead of doing the hard work to raise the academic performance of other students, however, the CRT-based solution is to limit or simply do away with AP courses altogether.[83] For example, the Culver City Unified School District in Los Angeles decided to eliminate Advanced Placement English classes after finding that the percentage of black students enrolled in these AP courses was 14% compared to 15% in the total student population and that the percentage of Hispanic students enrolled in those courses was only 13% compared to 37% in the student population.[84]

CRT is also being used to question whether assigning homework might be "racist". Homework is a necessary part of the education process and essential for academic rigor because, when properly used, homework reinforces what the students learn at school, develops independent study skills, teaches time management, and also enables teachers to see if students have actually learned what was taught outside a more formal and sporadic testing process.[85] However, there are disparities in the amount of time students in different ethnic groups spend on average in doing homework. "[T]he few studies examining racial and ethnic differences in homework time show that Black, and to a lesser extent Hispanic, students tend to spend less time on homework than their White peers, whereas Asian American students spend more time on homework than White students."[86] A study published in 2017 found that Asian students spent, on average, almost two hours per day on homework, while white and Hispanic students spent less than 50 minutes, and black students spent approximately 35 minutes per day on homework.[87]

The reasons for these disparities are manifold, just like the reasons for disparities in academic performance in general. However, a solution based on Critical Race Theory would simply eliminate or reduce the "homework gap" by eliminating or reducing homework. That is exactly the approach taken by the Los Angeles Unified School District in 2011 when it limited homework by requiring teachers to cap homework at 10 percent of the student's grade so that a student could theoretically refuse to do any homework in a class and still get a grade of A or A- (90%).[88]

Giving grades has itself been called racist due to statistical disparities. "White language supremacy in writing classrooms is due to the uneven and diverse linguistic legacies that everyone inherits, and the racialized white discourses that are used as standards, which give privilege to those students who embody those habits of white language already."[89] This attitude is shown towards all grading in an article written by a self-proclaimed "anti-racist educator"[90] who calls for completely dumping the present grading system and replacing it with a system similar to what was adopted in 2020 by the San Diego Unified School District.[91]

Standardized testing

There are substantial statistical disparities in standardized test scores between "students of color" and "Whites," whereby the group "Whites" also is considered to include Asians. It is much easier to eliminate the disparity in standardized testing by just getting rid of the tests than by doing the hard work to raise the level of academic performance and the skill needed to do well on the tests. Ibram X. Kendi, one of the most well-known voices in the Critical Race Theory camp, accordingly states:

> Standardized tests have become the most effective racist weapon ever devised to objectively degrade Black and Brown minds and legally exclude their bodies from prestigious schools.[92]

Both the Hispanic as well as the black achievement gaps express themselves especially in standardized testing results. For example, in 2020, the overall average score on the math Scholastic Aptitude Test (SAT) was 523 out of a possible 800. The average scores by race were 632 for Asians, 547 for Whites, 478 for Hispanics, and 454 for Blacks. A score of 530 is considered to be an accurate predictor for attaining a grade of C in a first-year college math course.[93]

The proportion of students reaching college readiness benchmarks also differs by race. Over half (59%) of white and four-fifths of Asian test takers met the college readiness math benchmark, compared to less than a quarter of black students and under a third of Hispanic or Latino students. As we show, there are similar patterns for English, but the gaps are not as stark.[94]

The National Education Association ("NEA") has long been critical of standardized tests.[95] The NEA asked in an open letter to the U.S. Department of Education, specifically due to COVID, that all "high-stakes" testing, i.e. tests that are important for admissions to high-end high schools and college, be stopped at least for the 2021/22 school year.[96] The College Board is responsible for designing the SAT and revising the SAT, especially to try to mitigate racial disparities in the scores. These efforts have not met with success. The revised test was administered for the first time for the 2016/17 school year, and the racial disparities in test scores continued with little change.

Since the revision did not have the intended effect of substantially reducing the racial disparities in college entrance exams, many universities have started to no longer require placement tests for the 2022/23 school year and instead only make them optional. The entire University of California system with ten campuses and the California State University system have gone even further and stopped

Group	Reading and Writing	Mathematics	Met Both Benchmarks
American Indian/Alaska Native	486	477	27%
Asian	569	612	70%
Black	479	462	20%
Latino	500	487	31%
Native Hawaiian/Pacific Islander	498	488	32%
White	565	553	59%

2017 Mean SAT Scores, and Percentage Meeting Benchmarks, by Race and Ethnicity[97]

considering standardized test scores even if they are

voluntarily submitted.[98] There is certainly no more effective or easier way to eliminate racial disparities in standardized testing than simply eliminating standardized testing altogether.

School discipline

There is no doubt that suspensions and expulsions affect academic performance for the simple reason that a student cannot keep pace with the class if the student is not in class.[99] There are distinct racial disparities in suspension rates. The following graph shows a general increase in suspension rates for all students, probably due in part to more widespread zero-tolerance policies and perhaps also a general loss of respect for authority in American culture. The graph especially shows an increase in per capita suspensions of black students from 6 % of black students suspended for at least one day in 1972-73 to a suspension rate of 15 % in 2006-07. There was also an increase in the racial disparity. Black students were suspended at twice the rate for white students in 1972-73 (6% compared to 3%), while the suspension rate for black students was three times higher in 2008-07 (15% compared to 5%).

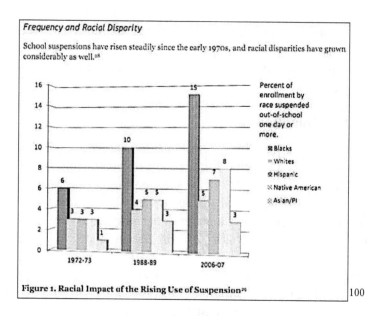

Frequency and Racial Disparity

School suspensions have risen steadily since the early 1970s, and racial disparities have grown considerably as well.[28]

Figure 1. Racial Impact of the Rising Use of Suspension[29]

100

The predictable solution based on Critical Race Theory would be to simply reduce or eliminate suspensions in general, and this is exactly the approach taken by California. "Today [27 September 2014] California becomes the first state in the nation to eliminate suspensions for its youngest children, and all expulsions of all students for minor misbehavior such as talking back, failing to have school materials and dress code violation."[101] California Assembly Bill 420 especially eliminated suspensions for "willful defiance," the basis for 43% of student suspensions in the state and also "the offense category with the most significant racial disparities."[102] The California Department of Education subsequently noted that "suspensions for willful defiance significantly decreased upon passage of this measure."[103] *Quelle surprise!* The state forbids suspensions for "willful defiance" and such suspensions decrease.

The California Department of Education explains the legislation eliminating willful defiance suspensions by expressly admitting that the reason for eliminating suspensions for willful defiance is the statistical disparity in the degree to which suspensions are imposed on so-called marginalized groups without addressing the possibility that such groups might have higher incidents of willful defiance.

> Research indicates that students of color; students with disabilities; and lesbian, gay, bisexual, transgender, queer, intersex, and asexual students are more likely to be suspended for low-level subjective offenses such as willful defiance.

The real issue is whether reducing or eliminating the racial disparities in suspension rates for willful defiance has any overall beneficial effect, especially for black and Hispanic students who the ban on suspensions was supposed to help. The expectation for the reduction of suspensions in lower grades for "willful defiance" was that it would result in a decrease in out-of-school suspensions, considered to be one of the most common forms of discipline in U.S. schools. However, an exhaustive analysis of data published in 2022 has shown that while bans on willful defiance suspensions, of course, reduced off-site suspensions for willful defiance, there was no effect on off-site suspensions overall. Bans on suspension for willful defiance were found to result in "no significant changes in overall rates of [off-site-suspensions] for White and Hispanic students" and the rate of off-site-suspensions for black students actually **increased** by approximately 26%.[104]

Is it just possible that a "broken windows" policy for discipline in school, especially in early grades, might reduce more serious problems in later years? There are countless studies that show a correlation in data between suspensions and other forms of tough discipline and poor academic performance.[105] This is not surprising since children who have serious disciplinary issues normally also have poor academic achievement. The real issue is how to prevent serious disciplinary issues because academic performance is better in an environment of academic discipline. Focusing on the teacher and not using cell phones in class, and turning in homework on time are minor steps that can have excellent results, but even such simple academic discipline is often lacking.

The findings in these studies also identify a statistical correlation between early discipline in school and subsequent crime and incarceration.

> Students who are quasi-randomly assigned to schools with higher conditional suspension rates are significantly more likely to be arrested and incarcerated as adults. This shows that early censure of school misbehavior causes increases in adult crime – that there is, in fact, a "school-to-prison pipeline."[106]

Such findings then serve as a basis for recommending easing school discipline. However, the statistical correlation does not necessarily show that "early censure of school misbehavior" actually **causes** increases in adult crime. The correlation may simply result from the fact that young people who engage in misbehavior resulting in suspensions or other serious disciplinary measures in school, are also more likely to engage in misbehavior as young adults. Every reader probably knew students who misbehaved in elementary school, were described at the time as headed to a life of crime and subsequently ended up in prison. Did early school punishment send these children down the path of perdition, or did other factors such as family situation, peer group pressure, or their own psychological makeup combined with a general lack of respect for authority lead to misbehavior in school and later on in life?

A very recent study published in January 2023 goes much further than identifying a statistical correlation between suspensions and poor academic performance.[107] This study looked at the effect over time of eliminating suspensions for "non-violent, disorderly conduct" in New York City public middle schools. The study's conclusion, quoted at some length below to also reflect the nuances, confirms what most people would intuitively sense:

> [A] reform eliminating suspensions for disorderly behavior in New York City led to significant gains in test scores for students in schools that were more affected by the change, relative to other schools. .., [W]e found no evidence of a trade-off between academic achievement and safety or disruptive behavior. Our results suggest that the gains were driven by cultural changes that benefited a wide range of students, even those who would not have been suspended under the previous regime. **By contrast, we rule out the possibility that any significant part of the gains came from the elimination of the direct impact of suspension on students who would themselves have been suspended.**
>
> Our results will be encouraging for those who seek to further reduce the reliance of schools on suspensions and other exclusionary punishments. The improvements we see in school culture contrast sharply with the stated justifications behind strict discipline policies and high suspension rates.
>
> However, we suggest caution when generalizing from our results to other types of discipline reform, especially those that target higher-level suspensions. The 2012 reform in New York City ... was the first step in easing a very strict discipline code. The

reform targeted the most discretionary suspensions, which were most likely to be perceived as overly harsh or unfair. By contrast, suspension may be necessary for more serious infractions, especially those that pose physical safety risks to other students. It is an open question whether changes to policies that target punishments for these infractions would lead to cultural and achievement gains similar to those we document here.

More broadly, this paper contributes to our understanding of the factors that make schools effective. It is well-documented that students' academic achievement can be improved by effective teachers (citation omitted), and by high-performing charter schools (citation omitted). We also have some appreciation for the package of practices that makes such schools effective; **This tends to include strict discipline, along with frequent teacher feedback, data-driven instruction, high-dosage tutoring, and increased instructional time** (citation omitted). However, our results suggest that instituting a strict discipline code by itself can be harmful to students, at least in the cross-section of New York City public schools that we study.[108] (emphasis added)

The general conclusion that can be drawn from all studies is that student misbehavior and corresponding disciplinary measures are much more complex than an analysis based on Critical Race Theory. Eliminating disciplinary tools and relaxing discipline overall based on racial disparities in discipline statistics does not address the underlying causes of student misbehavior in individual students but may well hurt other well-behaved students whose classroom instruction is disrupted by misbehavior.

1619 Project

When a school district considers banning the teaching of CRT as gospel in grades K-12, the argument is often made that CRT is not even taught in these grades and is, instead, only an esoteric topic in law schools. Although there are no courses (yet?) in American high schools or lower grade schools which actually teach Critical Race Theory as the curriculum, CRT "informs" education throughout the country. The effects are readily apparent in, for example, in the 1619 Project.

The 1619 Project was developed by the journalist Nikole Hannah-Jones together with writers at The New York Times to commemorate the 400th anniversary of the first African slaves landing in Virginia in 1619 after they were purchased by colonists from English pirates who had taken them off a Portuguese slave transport.[109] The 1619 Project is a prime example of how CRT looks at everything through the lens of race and also uses the technique of "storytelling." According to the 1619 Project, "one of the primary reasons the colonists decided to declare their independence from Britain was because they wanted to protect the institution of slavery."[110] Hannah-Jones argues that the American Revolution might well never have been fought "if [the Founding Fathers] had not believed that independence was required in order to ensure that slavery would continue."[111] In fact, Hannah-Jones appears to believe that she can identify the hidden motives of the Founding Fathers while accusing them of blatant hypocrisy in what they wrote for everyone to read in the Declaration of Independence and the Constitution. "The truth is that as much democracy as this nation has today, it has been borne on the backs of black resistance. Our founding fathers [sic] may not have actually believed in the ideals they espoused, but black people did."[112] In other words, Hannah-Jones ignores the words written by the

Founding Fathers after extensive debate and deliberation and finds that their real intent was just to preserve slavery.

Hannah-Jones's depiction of history, especially the American Revolution, is an excellent example of storytelling and has met with substantial criticism from historians. In a letter written to The New York Times editorial board shortly after the 1619 Project was first published, five professors of history wrote:

> On the American Revolution, for example – pivotal to any account of our history – the project asserts that the founders declared the colonies' independence from Britain "in order to ensure slavery would continue." If supportable, the allegation would be astounding – yet every statement offered to validate it is false.[113]

Professor Wilentz is quoted as saying to a reporter for *The Atlantic,* "To teach children that the American Revolution was fought in part to secure slavery would be giving a fundamental misunderstanding not only of what the American Revolution was all about but what America stood for and has stood for since the Founding." Hannah-Jones made what she considered to be a small concession to the criticism when she agreed that not all the colonists and instead only "some of the colonists" declared independence to preserve slavery.[114] However, she maintained the primary thesis expressed in the full title of her original article in the 1619 Project:

> Our founding ideals of liberty and equality were false when they were written. Black Americans fought to make them true. Without this struggle, America would have no democracy at all.[115]

Liberty in the form of individual rights and equality in the form of equality before the law were two completely new, revolutionary concepts when originally introduced. Although certainly not realized for all people living in the United States of America when the nation was first established and for more than a century afterwards, these concepts were just as valid when first embodied in our founding documents as they are now. American history has shown great progress to the point that the principles of individual liberty and equal protection under the law are now well established in American law and society in general. Despite the fundamental misrepresentations in the 1619 Project,[116] this curriculum developed by The Pulitzer Center on the basis of the 1619 Project is now being taught in more than 4,500 schools.[117]

3. Reparations

California Assembly Bill 3121 was passed and approved by Governor Newsom in 2020. AB 3121 established the "Task Force to Study and Develop Reparation Proposals for African Americans." The San Francisco Board of Supervisors also established the "San Francisco African American Reparations Advisory Committee," which issued a draft Reparations Plan in December 2022.[118] Among the more extravagant proposals (as numbered in the draft starting on pg. 2):

> 1.1   Provide a one-time, lump sum payment of $5 million to each eligible person.

> 1.2   Supplement African American income of lower income households to reflect the Area Median Income (AMI) for at least 250 years ($97,000 in 2022).

> 1.6   Finance a comprehensive debt forgiveness program that clears all educational, personal, credit card, payday loans, etc.

2.2   Guarantee continued funding for the Dream Keeper Down Payment Assistance Loan Program (DK-DALP) and convert the program from a loan to a forgivable grant over the course of 10 years, which shall be offered to eligible Reparations recipients, regardless of income.

In addition, the San Francisco draft plan includes countless race-based social programs, investment grants, hiring preferences, tax exemptions, etc. There is not enough money in the entire country to pay for the plan. The plan's blatant discrimination on the basis of race is clearly unconstitutional. The plan does not even require that an individual be a descendant of slaves. Under the eligibility requirements on page 30 of the plan, it is sufficient if a person is 18 years or older and has identified as "Black/African American" on public documents for at least ten years and any two criteria in a list of eight items. For example, an individual who moved to San Francisco before 1996 and who has personally been incarcerated during the "War on Drugs". Thus, a hypothetical migrant from Nigeria who arrived in San Francisco before 1996 and was convicted of dealing heroin would theoretically be eligible for a lump sum payment of $5 million and all other benefits in the plan.

Proposals for reparations are a direct reaction under CRT to the "wealth gap" between various ethnic groups. Although there are very rich and very poor individuals in all ethnic groups, there are large socio-economic discrepancies overall between ethnic groups. Statistics published by the Board of Governors of the Federal Reserve System in 2021 show as of 2018 that, the average household net worth of $ 142,520 for black households, $ 192,170 for Hispanic households, $ 952,910 for white households, and 1,039,350 for "other, non-Hispanic" households. The latter group consists, to a great extent, of Asian households.[119] The main argument in favor of reparations is that compensation is owed to descendants of slaves and persons hurt by Jim Crow laws by people who are descendants of ancestors who profited from slavery and Jim Crow and passed the wealth on to future generations.[120]

This argument ignores the fact that the wealth created by slavery, especially in the Confederate States, was largely destroyed by the Civil War.[121] The argument also ignores the sacrifices of the North in terms of wealth and lives during the Civil War as well as the fact that most Whites in the United States today are descendants of people who immigrated to America after the Civil War. One study shows that just since 1965 and 2015, immigrants during that period and their descendants increased the population of the United States by 72 million people to 325 million compared to 252 million people if there had been no immigration during this period.[122] This does not take into account the previous waves of immigration, especially during the period from 1880 to 1914, when over 20 million Europeans immigrated to the United States.[123]

Reparations raise serious concerns about the concept of equal protection under the law. Why should people who are descendants of slaves (and at the same time often slaveholders such as the black descendants of Thomas Jefferson) have a right to demand payment from the public coffers financed by descendants of people who came to America well after the Civil War and had nothing to do with slavery or, for that matter, Jim Crow laws? Why should the Asian American population, which never had anything to do with slavery or Jim Crow and many of whom came to the United States after the civil rights movement and prospered by hard work, be forced to transfer their wealth to members of another ethnic group? Reparations would create a chasm of hostility between ethnic groups in the United States that would take decades or even generations to close.

The only rationale for reparations is that a massive shift of wealth to Blacks could eliminate the statistical disparity between ethnic groups with regard to wealth. Reparations constitute just another, albeit massive quick fix for the supposedly "systemically racist" disparity in wealth between ethnic groups.

Chapter Summary

Critical Race Theory plays a major role in domestic policies in the United States of America. This is very apparent in the fields of crime and law enforcement, and education. Both areas have substantial racial disparities. Instead of focusing on the root causes and doing the difficult work to improve the lives of individuals in all ethnic groups, Critical Race Theory classifies the disparities as direct examples of racism and accordingly focuses on eliminating or reducing the statistical disparity, be it by decriminalizing activities or by eliminating the supposedly racist statistic itself, for example, getting rid of standardized testing. Critical Race Theory accordingly addresses the statistical "symptom" of socio-economic disparities between ethnic groups while playing down or completely ignoring the underlying causes of the disparities.

The practical consequence of Critical Race Theory is to reduce standards for behavior and achievement to the lowest common denominator. Critical Race Theory carried to an extreme leads to demands for a massive transfer of wealth in the form of reparations, a concept that could easily tear asunder American society. As will be shown, Critical Race Theory has already created a multi-billion dollar industry for the benefit of the purveyors of CRT.

1   Brandy Shufutinsky, "Who teaches the Teachers - University of California Schools of Education Indoctrinate Future Educators in Critical Race Theory and Related Ideologies", Legal Insurrection Foundation (January 9, 2023), https://criticalrace.org/app/uploads/2023/01/UC-Schools-of-Education-Report-1.pdf.

2   SB 1495 in Section 52, amending section 10153.2 (a) (1) (A) (i) of the Business and Professions Code, https://legiscan.com/CA/text/SB1495/2021.

3   King County, WA resolution 20-08 adopted by the King County Board of Health on Jun 18, 2020, https://mrsc.org/getmedia/cfd050db-4a7a-4913-a9e1-39d27d64ba82/k5BOHr20-08.pdf.aspx.

4   Ethan C. Campbell, "Technical report on bicycle infractions in Seattle (2003-2020): Methodology and preliminary findings on racial disparities", pg. 1, https://ipmba.org/images/uploads/Technical_report_on_bicycle_infractions_in_Seattle_(2003-2020).pdf.

5   Ibid., pg. 1 in the Executive Summary.

6   Sopohie Kasakova, "Seattle Bike Helmet Rule Is Dropped Amid Racial Justice Concerns", New York Times, (February 18, 2022), https://www.nytimes.com/2022/02/18/us/seattle-bicycle-helmet.html.

7   Josh Cohen, "King County Board of Health repeals decades-old helmet law", Crosscut.com, (February 17, 2022), https://crosscut.com/politics/2022/02/king-county-board-health-repeals-decades-old-helmet-law.

8   Guy Oron, "As Sound Transit Weighs Future of Fare Ambassador Program, Data Shows History of Racial Disparities in Fare Enforcement", The Urbanist (2022), https://www.theurbanist.org/2022/01/18/as-sound-transit-weighs-future-of-fare-ambassador-program-data-shows-history-of-racial-disparities-in-fare-enforcement/.

9   Guy Oron, "Tap below: Sound Transit to reintroduce fare enforcement in September, despite past racially disproportionate fines and charges", Real Change (June 1, 2922): This paper contains an extensive summary of various studies. https://www.realchangenews.org/news/2022/06/01/tap-below-sound-transit-reintroduce-fare-enforcement-september-despite-past-racially.

10   Ibid.

¹¹   Colin Porter, "Bail Discrimination: Racial Disparities in the United States Bail Determination Process", Clark University – Clark Digital Commons (2021), pg. 17, https://commons.clarku.edu/cgi/viewcontent.cgi?article=1074&context=sps_masters_papers.

¹²   Ibid., pg. 21

¹³   Ibid.

¹⁴   Gersh Kuntzman, " 'Jaywalking While Black': Final 2019 Numbers Show Race-Based NYPD Crackdown Continues", in STREETSBLOG NYC (January 27, 2020), available at https://nyc.streetsblog.org/2020/01/27/jaywalking-while-black-final-2019-numbers-show-race-based-nypd-crackdown-continues/.

¹⁵   Ibid.

¹⁶   Ibid.

¹⁷   Gersh Kuntzman, "NYPD's Racial Bias in 'Jaywalking' Tickets Continues into 2020" in STREETSBLOG NYC (May 7, 2020), https://nyc.streetsblog.org/2020/05/07/nypds-racial-bias-in-jaywalking-tickets-continues-into-2020/.

¹⁸   Dave Colon, "STREETSBLOG GETS ACTION: Council Will Probe NYPD's Biased 'Jaywalking' Enforcement" (January 27, 2020), https://nyc.streetsblog.org/2020/01/27/streetsblog-gets-action-council-will-probe-nypds-biased-jaywalking-enforcement/.

¹⁹   California Assemblyman Phil Tin (D San Francisco) who authored legislation to weaken California's jaywalking law quoted in "Everyone 'Jaywalks,' But Black Pedestrians Are Disproportionately Cited. Will California 'Decriminalize Walking?" in LAist (September 8, 2021), https://laist.com/news/transportation/jaywalking-pedestrian-ab-1238-traffic-safety.

²⁰   Erin Heft, "Pedestrian deaths account for over 25% of all California traffic fatalities, officials say", KCRA3, (October 17, 2022), https://www.kcra.com/article/pedestrian-deaths-increase-in-california/41658979.

²¹   Matthew A. Raifman and Ernani F. Choma, "Disparities in Activity and Traffic Fatalities by Race/Ethnicity", in American Journal of Preventive Medicine, volume 63 issue 2 (June 7, 2022). pp. 160 – 167, https://www.ajpmonline.org/article/S0749-3797(22)00155-6/fulltext.

²²   Gabriel L. Schwartz and Jaquelyn L. Jahn, "Mapping fatal police violence across U.S. metropolitan areas: Overall rates and racial/ethnic inequities, 2013-2017", in PLOS ONE (June 24, 2020),

https://journals.plos.org/plosone/article?id=10.1371/journal.pone.02296
86.

23   Danielle Haynes, "Study: Black Americans 3 times more
likely to be killed by police", UPI (June 24, 2020),
https://www.upi.com/Top_News/US/2020/06/24/Study-Black-
Americans-3-times-more-likely-to-be-killed-by-
police/6121592949925/.

24   Video of President Obama, available on YouTube at
https://www.youtube.com/watch?v=Yt_g5JPdP8Y.

25   Acquittal reported e.g. by CNN on July 14, 2014 "George
Zimmerman found not guilty of murder in Trayvon Martin's death",
available at https://www.cnn.com/2013/07/13/justice/zimmerman-
trial/index.html; Barbara Lisbon, "Eyewitness describes Trayvon
Martin's fatal struggle to Florida jury", 28 June 2013, Reuters, available
at https://www.reuters.com/article/us-usa-florida-shooting/eyewitness-
describes-trayvon-martins-fatal-struggle-to-florida-jury-
idUSBRE95Q0EE20130628.

26   Black Lives Matter "Herstory", available at
https://blacklivesmatter.com/herstory/.

27   Douglas Wiley, "Why Officer Darren Wilson wasn't indicted"
(November 24, 2014) in Police1, available at
https://www.police1.com/ferguson/articles/why-officer-darren-wilson-
wasnt-indicted-b3DTGpEkDemKS2P5/.

28   Department of Justice Report Regarding the Criminal
Investigation into the Shooting of Michael Brown by Ferguson,
Missouri Police Officer Darren Wilson (March 4, 2015),
https://www.justice.gov/sites/default/files/opa/press-
releases/attachments/2015/03/04/doj_report_on_shooting_of_michael_
brown_1.pdf.

29   Table 43 for 2019 available at https://ucr.fbi.gov/crime-in-the-
u.s/2019/crime-in-the-u.s.-2019/topic-pages/tables/table-43.

30   "Police departments in the US: Explained" published on
August 13, 2020, updated on April 28, 2021, published online in USA
FACTS, https://usafacts.org/articles/police-departments-explained/.

31   Allen C. Beck, "Race and Ethnicity of Violent Crime
Offenders and Arrestees, 2018", U.S. Department of Justice, Bureau of
Statistics (2021), available at
https://bjs.ojp.gov/content/pub/pdf/revcoa18.pdf.

32   "Officer's chokehold triggered Eric Garner's death, medical
examiner testifies", CBS News (May 15, 2019),

https://www.cbsnews.com/news/eric-garners-death-triggered-by-chokehold-medical-examiner-testifies-in-officer-daniel-pantaleo-trial-2019-05-15/.

[33]   G. Wesley Clark, M.D., "A Medical Perspective on the Garner Tragedy", in American Thinker (December 8, 2014), https://www.americanthinker.com/articles/2014/12/a_medical_perspective_on_the_garner_tragedy.html.

[34]   "hypoxia" described online by the Cleveland Clinic at https://my.clevelandclinic.org/health/diseases/23063-hypoxia#:~:text=Hypoxia%20is%20low%20levels%20of,you%20at%20risk%20for%20hypoxia; "hypoxemia" described online by the Cleveland Clinic at https://my.clevelandclinic.org/health/diseases/17727-hypoxemia.

[35]   The Eric Garner case and other prominent cases, starting with the killing of Trayvon Martin in 2012 which led to the founding of Black Lives Matter, are discussed in detail in the book by David Horowitz, *I Can't Breathe – How a Racial Hoax is Killing America*, Regenery Publishing (2021).

[36]   Associated Press, "Chicago police will no longer be allowed to chase people on foot" (June 22, 2022), NPR, available at https://www.npr.org/2022/06/22/1106654201/chicago-police-will-no-longer-be-allowed-to-chase-people-on-foot.

[37]   Angela Caputo, Jennifer Richards, Jason Meisner, "Third of police shootings started with foot chases, Tribune analysis finds" (September 7, 2016), Chicago Tribune, available at https://www.chicagotribune.com/investigations/ct-chicago-police-shooting-foot-chase-met-20160907-story.html.

[38]   Ibid.

[39]   Baltimore Police Department Policy 1505, https://www.baltimorepolice.org/transparency/bpd-policies/1505-foot-pursuits.

[40]   The City of Portland, Oregon, Police Bureau Directive No. 0630.15, Foot Pursuits, https://www.portlandoregon.gov/police/article/798199.

[41]   Peter Nickeas, "More law enforcement departments are limiting risky police changes", CNN (March 2022), https://www.cnn.com/2022/03/08/us/police-restricting-pursuits/index.html.

[42]   RCW 10.116.060, available at https://app.leg.wa.gov/RCW/default.aspx?cite=10.116.060.

⁴³   Austin Jenkins, "See Ya! Washington Police Sat Drivers Aren't Stopping for Them, Cite Pursuit Restrictions", Northwest Public Broadcasting (May 27, 2022), https://www.nwpb.org/2022/05/27/see-ya-washington-police-say-drivers-arent-stopping-for-them-cite-pursuit-restrictions/.

⁴⁴   Ibid.

⁴⁵   Assembly Bill 742 in the 2023-2024 regular session of the California Legislature, https://legiscan.com/CA/text/AB742/id/2696383.

⁴⁶   Allen C. Beck, "Race and Ethnicity of Violent Crime Offenders and Arrestees, 2018", U.S. Department of Justice, Bureau of Statistics (2021), available at https://bjs.ojp.gov/content/pub/pdf/revcoa18.pdf.

⁴⁷   United States Attorney General Robert H. Jackson in a speech on April 1, 1940 to United State Attorneys, text of speech in Robert H. Jackson, "The Federal Prosecutor" in Journal of Criminal Law and Criminology, Vol. 31, issue 1 (Summer 1940), pg. 3, https://scholarlycommons.law.northwestern.edu/cgi/viewcontent.cgi?article=2931&context=jclc.

⁴⁸   This movement is discussed in more detail in Daniel Fryer, "Race, Reform, & Progressive Prosecution", Journal of Criminal Law and Criminology, Vol. 110, issue 4 (Fall 1940), pp. 769 – 802, https://scholarlycommons.law.northwestern.edu/cgi/viewcontent.cgi?article=7681&context=jclc.

⁴⁹   President Barack Obama, speech at the University of Illinois, September 7, 2018, transcript available on website of NBC station 5 in Chicago, https://www.nbcchicago.com/news/local/obama-university-of-illinois-full-speech/173866/.

⁵⁰   Megan Cassidy, Mallory Moench, Joshua Sharpe, "Chesa Boudin ousted as San Francisco district attorney in historic recall", San Francisco Chronicle (June 7, 2022), https://www.sfchronicle.com/election/article/Chesa-Boudin-ousted-as-San-Francisco-District-17226641.php.

⁵¹   Heather Pickerell, "Critical Race Theory & Power: The Case for Progressive Prosecution," Harvard BlackLetter Law Journal (April 1, 2020) pp. 73 – 89, https://papers.ssrn.com/sol3/papers.cfm?abstract_id=3658729.

⁵²   Press release by George Gascón's campaign website, "George Gascón takes Oath of Office and Institutes Sweeping Reforms to Transform the Largest Criminal Justice Jurisdiction in America"

(December 8, 2020), https://georgegascon.org/campaign-news/george-gascon-takes-oath-of-office-and-institutes-sweeping-reforms-to-transform-the-largest-criminal-justice-jurisdiction-in-america/.

53   Parker Thayer, "Living Room Pundit's Guide to Soros District Attorneys", in Capital Research Center (January 18, 2022), https://capitalresearch.org/article/living-room-pundits-guide-to-soros-district-attorneys/.

54   Ibid., see also, Joseph Simonson, "George Soros-backed prosecutor in St. Louis oversees 50-year-high murder rate", *Washington Examiner* (January 31, 2023), https://www.washingtonexaminer.com/news/st-louis-murder-rate.

55   Lawrence Mower and Emily L. Mahoney, "DeSantis removes Hillsborough County State Attorney Andrew Warren", *Tampa Bay Times* (August 4, 2022), https://www.tampabay.com/news/florida-politics/2022/08/04/desantis-suspends-hillsborough-county-state-attorney-andrew-warren/.

56   Delgado/Stefancic, pp. 120-124.

57   U.S. Criminal Justice Data, The Sentencing Project, https://www.sentencingproject.org/research/us-criminal-justice-data/.

58   Ibid.

59   Ibid.

60   Ibid.

61   "The 50th Anniversary of the August 7th Marin County Courthouse Rebellion", The Freedom Archives, https://freedomarchives.org/projects/the-50th-anniversary-of-the-august-7th-marin-county-courthouse-rebellion/.

62   Leslie Veliz, "The Real Reason Angela Davis Was Acquitted of Murder", *The Grunge* (July 15, 2022), https://www.grunge.com/928565/the-real-reason-angela-davis-was-acquitted-of-murder/.

63   Keeranga-Yahmahita Taylor, "The Emerging Movement for Police and Prison Abolition" in *Black Agenda Report* (May 12, 2021), https://www.blackagendareport.com/emerging-movement-police-and-prison-abolition.

64   Jessica Eaglin and Danyelle Solomon, "Reducing Racial and Ethnic Disparities in Jails – Recommendation for Local Practice", (June 25, 2015) The Brennan Center for Justice, https://www.brennancenter.org/our-work/policy-solutions/reducing-racial-and-ethnic-disparities-jails.

65   Hope Corman and Naci Mocan, "Carrots, Sticks and Broken Windows", National Bureau of Economic Research, paid for by the Independent Budget Office of New York City, (July 2002) pg. 14, https://www.nber.org/system/files/working_papers/w9061/w9061.pdf.

66   Ibid., pg. 22.

67   Sarah Burnett, "For world, Floyd's death was about race. Why not the trials?", AP News (February 24, 2022, https://apnews.com/article/death-of-george-floyd-ahmaud-arbery-george-floyd-race-and-ethnicity-04ad7633c49f94475d5c9f5c5a381c24.

68   Rick Rojas, Neelam Bohra, Eliza Fawcett, "What We Know About Tyre Nichols's Lethal Encounter With Memphis Police", *The New York Times*, (February 12, 2023) at https://www.nytimes.com/article/tyre-nichols-memphis-police-dead.html.

69   Results of the IPSOS poll conducted as a survey of the American general population in interviews conducted between April 26 and May 4, 2021, Section 12, first question, pg. 18, https://www.ipsos.com/sites/default/files/ct/news/documents/2021-05/Topline%20Axios%20Hard%20Truth%20Civil%20Rights%200052321.pdf.

70   Morrisey, Hutchinson, Winsler, "Family income, school attendance, and academic achievement in elementary school", National Library of Medicine at the National Institute of Health (NIH), (March 2014), available at https://pubmed.ncbi.nlm.nih.gov/23914750/#:~:text=Low%20family%20income%20is%20associated,income%20impacts%20children's%20academic%20success.

71   W. Bradford Wilcox, "Strong Families, Better Student Performance: The More Things Change, the More They Remain the Same", Institute for Family Studies (August 16, 2022), https://ifstudies.org/blog/strong-families-better-student-performance-the-more-things-change-the-more-they-remain-the-same.

72   Natasha Dagys Pajoluk, "Sibling Relationship Predictors of Academic Achievement in Adolescents", dissertation University of California, Berkeley (2013), pg. 24, https://citeseerx.ist.psu.edu/document?repid=rep1&type=pdf&doi=4fbeeb7ccf21f9d5f2c339e5e0807cfeb761bab9.

73   Daniel Voyer and Susan D. Voyer, "Gender differences in scholastic achievement: A meta-analysis", Psychological Bulletin Vol. 140 No. 4 (2014) pp. 1174-1208, https://www.apa.org/pubs/journals/releases/bul-a0036620.pdf.

74   Xitao Fen, Michael J. Chen, "Academic Achievement of Rural School Students: A Multi-Year Comparison with Their Peers in Suburban and Urban Schools", Utah State University (1998), https://files.eric.ed.gov/fulltext/ED418829.pdf.

75   Anna J. Egalite, "How Family Background Influences Student Achievement", Education Next, Vol. 16 No. 2, 70-78 (2016), https://www.educationnext.org/how-family-background-influences-student-achievement/.

76   Amanda Gardner, "Does obesity affect school performance?" CNN Health online (June 14, 2012), https://www.cnn.com/2012/06/14/health/obesity-affect-school-performance/index.html .

77   Lauren Camera, "Achievement Gap Between White and Black Students Still Gaping" (January 13, 2016) in U.S.News online, https://www.usnews.com/news/blogs/data-mine/2016/01/13/achievement-gap-between-white-and-black-students-still-gaping.

78   Karen Abrams and Fanying Kong, "The Variables Most Closely Associated With Academic Achievement: A Review of the Research Literature", in PR>I Progressive Research Institute of Nebraska (September 2012), https://www.usnews.com/news/blogs/data-mine/2016/01/13/achievement-gap-between-white-and-black-students-still-gaping .

79   Georgia Thompson, Jane Moore, Sabrina Jones, "8 Great Ways to Close the Achievement Gap", in Istation (2019), https://www.cde.state.co.us/coloradoliteracy/istationmarch2019newsletter

80   Ibid., pg. 2

81   "NYC Schools to End Gifted & Talented Program in Favor of 'Accelerated Learning' Model", NBC 4 in New York (October 7, 2021, updated October 9, 2021), https://www.nbcnewyork.com/news/local/nyc-schools-to-eliminate-controversial-gifted-talented-classes/3313300/.

82   Alina Adams, "NYC Parents Rage: With No G&T Qualifying Test, Selection Process Is Chaos", in The 74 (August 8, 2022), https://www.the74million.org/article/nyc-parents-rage-with-no-gt-qualifying-test-selection-process-is-chaos/.

83   Betsy McCaughey, "Racial-equity warriors are hurting the disadvantaged by dumbing-down schools", New York Post (March 10,

2022), https://nypost.com/2022/03/10/racial-equity-warriors-are-actually-hurting-the-disadvantaged/.

[84]   Sara Randazzo, "To Increase Equity, School Districts Eliminate Honors Classes", *The Wall Street Journal* (February 17, 2023), https://www.wsj.com/articles/to-increase-equity-school-districts-eliminate-honors-classes-d5985dee?st=ls334z8xto65lek&reflink=desktopwebshare_permalink.

[85]   "11 Awesome Homework Benefits for Students" published online in TutorBin (October 11, 2022), https://tutorbin.com/blog/11-awesome-homework-benefits-for-students.

[86]   Allison Dunatchik and Hyunloon Park, "Racial and Ethnic Differences in Homework Time among U.S. Teens", in *Sage Journals* (June 11, 2022), https://journals.sagepub.com/doi/full/10.1177/07311214221101422.

[87]   Michael Hansen and Diana Quintaro, "Analyzing 'the homework gap' among high school students", Brookings Institution (August 10, 2017), https://www.brookings.edu/blog/brown-center-chalkboard/2017/08/10/analyzing-the-homework-gap-among-high-school-students/.

[88]   Simone Wilson, "LAUSD Declares Homework Racist, Classist", *LA Weekly* (June 24, 2011) https://www.laweekly.com/lausd-declares-homework-racist-classist/.

[89]   Prof. Asao Inoue, quoted in "Arizona State University professor says traditional grading system is 'racist' and demands an end to 'white supremacy' by grading papers based on EFFORT: Some students have 'privilege' because they 'embody those habits of white language already' " *Daily Mail* (November 9, 2021), https://www.dailymail.co.uk/news/article-10183499/Arizona-State-University-prof-says-grading-racist-based-labor.html.

[90]   Ken Shelton and Nadia Razi, "Grading Can Be Capitalist, Racist and Exploitative", in Age of Awareness (June 14, 2021), https://medium.com/age-of-awareness/grading-is-capitalist-racist-and-exploitative-b40d309596c3.

[91]   San Diego Unified School District Administrative Regulation ("AR") 5121 which retains the grades A, B, C, D and F while redefining them in a range from A meaning "Exceeding content area standards" to F meaning "Little to no progress towards meeting content area standards", available at https://cdn5-ss18.sharpschool.com/UserFiles/Servers/Server_27732394/File/Grading%20Policy/AR%205121%20Grades%20Evaluation%20of%20Student%20Achievement%20Rev.%2010-20%20FINAL.pdf.

⁹²   Ibram C. Kendi, "Testimony in Support of the Working Group Recommendation to #SuspendTheTest," Boston Coalition for Education Equity (October 21, 2020), https://www.bosedequity.org/blog/read-ibram-x-kendis-testimony-in-support-of-the-working-group-recommendation-to-suspendthetest.

⁹³   Ember Smith and Richard V. Reeves, "SAT math scores mirror and maintain racial inequity" (December 1, 2020), The Brookings Institution, available at https://www.brookings.edu/blog/up-front/2020/12/01/sat-math-scores-mirror-and-maintain-racial-inequity/.

⁹⁴   Ibid.

⁹⁵   For example, Carol A. Norman, "measurement and Testing: An NEA Perspective. NEA Research Memo" (1980), https://files.eric.ed.gov/fulltext/ED213762.pdf.

⁹⁶   National Education Association, "Beyond the Bubble" (May 2021), https://www.nea.org/sites/default/files/2021-05/BeyondTheBubble.pdf.

⁹⁷   Scott Jaschik, "New SAT, Old Gaps on Race", Inside Higher Ed (September 27, 2017), https://www.insidehighered.com/news/2017/09/27/scores-new-sat-show-large-gaps-race-and-ethnicity.

⁹⁸   Michael T. Nietzel, "More Thanks 80% of Four-Year Colleges Won't Require Standardized Tests for Fall 2023 Admissions", in Forbes (November 15, 2022), https://www.forbes.com/sites/michaeltnietzel/2022/11/15/more-than-80-of-four-year-colleges-wont-require-standardized--tests-for-fall-2023-admissions/?sh=960e3f97fb96.

⁹⁹   Amity L Noltemeyer, Rose Marie Ward, Caven Mcloughlin, "Relationship Between School Suspension and Student Outcome: A Meta-Analysis" (2015) School Psychology Review vol. 44 no. 2 (2015), pp. 224-240, https://edsource.org/wp-content/uploads/2018/09/Noltemeyer_Ward_2015_Meta-Analysis.pdf.

¹⁰⁰   Daniel J. Losen, "Discipline Policies, Successfrul Schools, and Racial Justice," National Education Policy Center at the Schoo9l of Education, University of Colorado Boulder (October 2011), pg. 4, https://nepc.colorado.edu/sites/default/files/NEPC-SchoolDiscipline.pdf.

¹⁰¹   ACLU Northern California, "California Enacts First-in-the-Nation Law to Eliminate Student Suspensions for Minor Misbehavior" (September 27, 2014) press release, https://www.aclunc.org/news/california-enacts-first-nation-law-

eliminate-student-suspensions-minor-
misbehavior#:~:text=Sacramento%20%E2%80%93%20Today%20Cali
fornia%20becomes%20the,Gov.

[102]   Ibid.

[103]   California Department of Education, "State Guidance for New
Laws on Discipline" (August 19, 2021),
https://www.cde.ca.gov/nr/el/le/yr21ltr0819.asp.

[104]   Bui Wang, "The Impact of Suspension Reforms on Discipline
Outcomes: Evidence from California High Schools", AERA Open in
SAGE journals (January 26, 2022),
https://journals.sagepub.com/doi/10.1177/23328584211068067.

[105]   For example, Andrew Bacher-Hicks, Stephen B. Billings,
David J. Deming, "The School to Prison Pipeline – Long Run Impact of
School Suspensions on Adult Crime" Working Paper 26257 published
by National Bureau of Economic Research (September 2017),
https://www.nber.org/system/files/working_papers/w26257/w26257.pd
f.

[106]   Ibid., pg. 27.

[107]   Ashley C. Craig, David C. Martin, "Discipline Reform, School
Culture, and Student Achievement" (January 2023),
https://sites.lsa.umich.edu/ashcraig/wp-
content/uploads/sites/716/2021/06/suspensions_paper.pdf

[108]   Ibid., pp. 43. 44.

[109]   Nikole Hannah-Jones, "The 1619 Project", The New York
Times Magazine (August 18, 2019), pg. 16,
https://pulitzercenter.org/sites/default/files/full_issue_of_the_1619_proj
ect.pdf.

[110]   Ibid., pg. 18.

[111]   Ibid.

[112]   Ibid., pg. 26

[113]   Letter by Professors Victoria Bynum, James M. McPherson,
James Oakes, Sean Wilentz and Gordon S. Wood (December 4, 2019),
https://www.cbs17.com/wp-content/uploads/sites/29/2021/07/NYT-
1619-Letter-Bennet.pdf.

[114]   Becket Adams, "Seven months later, 1619 Project leader
admits she got it wrong", Washington Examiner (March 12, 2020),
available at https://www.washingtonexaminer.com/opinion/seven-
months-later-1619-project-leader-admits-she-got-it-wrong.

[115]   Nikole Hannah-Jones, "The 1619 Project" (2019). The New
Times Magazine, pg. 14.

[116] See e.g., Leslie M. Harris, "I Helped Fact-Check the 1619 Project. The Times Ignored Me", Politico (March 5, 2020), https://www.politico.com/news/magazine/2020/03/06/1619-project-new-york-times-mistake-122248.

[117] Hannah Farrow, "The 1619 Project curriculum taught in over 4,500 schools — Frederick County Public Schools has the option", in Medill News Service (July 21, 2020), https://dc.medill.northwestern.edu/blog/2020/07/21/the-1619-project-curriculum-taught-in-over-4500-schools-frederick-county-public-schools-has-the-option/.

[118] Draft Reparations Plan, https://sf.gov/sites/default/files/2023-01/HRC%20Reparations%202022%20Report%20Final_0.pdf.

[119] Adilya Aladangady and Akila Forde, "Wealth Inequality and the Racial Wealth Gap", Federal Reserve (October 22, 2021), https://www.federalreserve.gov/econres/notes/feds-notes/wealth-inequality-and-the-racial-wealth-gap-20211022.html, detail data at https://www.federalreserve.gov/econres/notes/feds-notes/wealth-inequality-and-the-racial-wealth-gap-accessible-20211022.htm#fig1.

[120] Rashawn Ray and Andre Perry, "Why we need reparations for Black Americans", in Policy 2020 – Brookings Institution (April 15, 2020), https://www.brookings.edu/policy2020/bigideas/why-we-need-reparations-for-black-americans/.

[121] Joshua Rosenbloom, Brandon Dupont, "Impact of the US Civil War on southern wealth holders", VoxEU – CEPR (June 19, 2016), https://cepr.org/voxeu/columns/impact-us-civil-war-southern-wealth-holders#:~:text=The%20Civil%20War%20and%20emancipation%20destroyed%20an%20immense%20amount%20of,top%20of%20the%20wealth%20distribution.

[122] "Modern Immigration Wave Brings 59 Million to U.S., Driving Population Growth and Change Through 2065", Pew Research Institute (September 28, 2015), https://www.pewresearch.org/hispanic/2015/09/28/modern-immigration-wave-brings-59-million-to-u-s-driving-population-growth-and-change-through-2065/.

[123] Philip Martin, "The Global Challenge of Managing Migration", Population Bulletin Vol. 68, No. 2 (November 2013), https://www.prb.org/wp-content/uploads/2014/05/Population-bulletin-2013-68-2-global-migration.pdf.

Chapter VI

The Scam

Critical Race Theory is a divisive political ideology. CRT is inherently racist (under the traditional definition) because CRT uses the criterion of race to classify everyone in the country as a member of the "oppressor" class or the "oppressed" class. This serves to build a political movement using an emotional "us versus them" appeal, a ploy that has been standard practice for despots throughout history. But is calling Critical Race Theory a "scam" perhaps going a step too far? According to The Britannica Dictionary, a scam is "a dishonest way to make money by deceiving people."[1] The definitions in other dictionaries are comparable. The defining elements of the term "scam" are deception and making money.

There can be no doubt, after the discussion in the previous chapters, that Critical Race Theory is extremely deceptive. The fundamental assumption of fact in CRT, according to which racism is everywhere in America and the normal way we do business, is demonstrably false. The redefinition of "racism" in CRT to mean "racial prejudice + power" applies the highly pejorative term "racist" to all Whites and, for that matter, to anyone who disagrees with the ideology of CRT, while CRT also argues on the basis of the new definition that people of color cannot be racist. The philosophical foundation of CRT in the dialectic approach is completely simple-minded, just as is the case with the pseudo-intellectual concepts of "interest convergence" and "intersectionality," not to mention the blatantly racist (in the traditional sense of the term) "voice of color thesis". Critical Race Theory implicitly admits the use of deception when CRT praises "storytelling" as a tool for advancing the CRT political movement.

Should all proponents of CRT, therefore, be considered to be personally dishonest? This conclusion would indeed be a step too far. Just as there were snake oil salesmen in the Old West as well as purveyors of miracle treatments and food supplements today who, in good faith, believe in the efficacy of their products, there are certainly many proponents of CRT today who are genuinely convinced that CRT can lead to better understanding the issues of race in America. There are certainly some proponents of CRT who, at least in the meantime, recognize full well that the CRT emperor has no clothes yet continue to exploit the ideology for personal benefit.

Is Critical Race Theory just an "academic" pursuit on the part of self-absorbed professors, or has CRT become a business that generates billions of dollars for people who sow racial animosity for a living? To get the answer: **Follow the money!**

Black Lives Matter.

The most obvious money trail reported in the press leads to Black Lives Matter Global Networks Foundation, Inc. ("BLMGNF"), the central unit in the Black Lives Matter ("BLM") movement, which included many local branches in the USA and other countries. The BLM movement started in 2013 after George Zimmerman was acquitted in the killing of Trayvon Martin in 2012.[2] One of the main founders was Patrisse Cullors. The BLM movement experienced more growth after Michael Brown was killed in Ferguson, Missouri, in 2014. By 2017, the founders of the BLM movement decided to establish a parent entity where donations to the BLM movement could be pooled, and BLMGNF was established. The BLM movement and specifically the BLMGNF organization became prominent after the death of George Floyd in May 2020, and the new prominence reportedly brought in approximately $90 million in donations, with about one-quarter of that amount redistributed to local chapters of BLM and other organizations.[3] The IRS Form 990 (pg. 1 line 12) filed by BLMGNF for the financial year July 1, 2020 to June 30, 2021[4] shows total revenue during that time period of $ 79,644,823.

However, with the money came greed, personal enrichment, mismanagement, waste, litigation, and suspicion of criminal misuse of donated funds. Form 990 lists in line 10a an asset consisting of real property having a value of $ 5,998,781 before depreciation.[5] BLMGNF purchased a 6,500 sq. ft. home in Los Angeles with at least six bedrooms for almost $ 6,000,000 in October 2020 to supposedly "serve as housing and studio space for recipients of the Black Joy Creators Fellowship."[6] A report in the New York Post stated that the price was 250% higher than for comparable homes in the neighborhood.[7] After criticism in the press about three private house purchases, Patrisse Cullors resigned as the Executive Director in May 2021.[8] The audit report of BLMGNF[9] lists under Note 8 on pg. 15 the following questionable transactions with related parties:

- A sibling of the Executive Director [the older brother of Patrisse Cullors] owned a security and protection company, which was paid $840,993 for security services during the year ended June 30, 2021.

- A related party to the Executive Director of BLMGNF was a board member of M4BJ operating as Black Lives Matter Canada, which was granted $8,024,626 during fiscal year ended June 30, 2021.

The organizational structure of the Black Lives Matters movement changed in 2020 when the individual chapters were spun off into a new entity, "Black Lives Matters Grassroots." BLMGNF had developed a spin-off plan in order to transition to the new organizational structure.

However, turf wars quickly arose between the two organizations since BLMGNF and its sole director Shalomyah Bowers took over after the former leadership under Patrisse Cullors resigned. Bowers already had a close relationship with BLMGNF which paid $ 2,167,894 for consulting services in the financial year 2020/21.[10] BLMGNF also paid Trap Heals LLC, a firm owned by the father of Patrisse Cullors's son, $ 969,459 for media services in the same period.[11] Black Lives Matters Grassroots finally issued an open letter to BLMGNF demanding that the organization turn over financial assets and intellectual property since BLM Grassroots argued that the chapters and other organizations were the true representatives of the BLM movement. The open letter states as its demands:

> We demand the immediate transference of all decision-making and representative power and platforms (including the website and social media) to Black Lives Matter Grassroots and that you stop representing Black Lives Matter in any way. We further demand an immediate end to any major spending or purchases and that all legally and contractually required spending be made public and transparent. We demand that all assets be transferred to Black Lives Matter Grassroots and that BLM GNF be formally and legally dissolved.[12]

The conflict is now the subject of a lawsuit after BLM Grassroots filed a complaint before the Superior Court in Los Angeles County accusing BLMGNF of fraud and other improper conduct, much of which also sounds like violations of criminal law based on the statements in the civil complaint.[13] The lawyers are the only group that, with certainty, will benefit substantially from the donations given to both BLMGNF as well as BLM Grassroots.

Diversity, Equity & Inclusion ("DEI")

The Civil Rights Act of 1964 put the final, main nail in the coffin of Jim Crow. This statute expressly prohibited racial discrimination in employment, public accommodations, etc. Countless cases have been brought against employers alleging illegal racial discrimination as well as other forms of discrimination. During the 1960s, the 1970s, and well into the 1980s, anti-discrimination consulting involved primarily lawyers with specialized knowledge in civil rights law who trained managers and especially personnel departments about the do's and don'ts under civil rights law (compliance training). Today, no sane employer would risk the immense damages and legal costs involved in being sued for intentional racial discrimination, not to mention the reputational harm.

Soon after cases started to be filed with the courts based on racial discrimination in employment, it became apparent that discrimination did not just consist of intentionally excluding people from jobs based on race. Discrimination could also occur if non-job related qualifications for employment were introduced that disproportionately excluded people of different races from employment, i.e. if there was a "disparate impact", whether intended or not. The U.S. Supreme Court established the basis for "disparate impact analysis" in the leading case *Griggs v. Duke Power Co., 401 U.S. 424 (1971)*. The facts of the case, as described by the Supreme Court in its own words, clearly show how the introduction of a policy that, on its face, appears to be fair can violate the Civil Rights Act:

> [T]he Company openly discriminated on the basis of race in the hiring and assigning of employees at its Dan River plant. The plant was organized into five operating departments: (1) Labor, (2) Coal Handling, (3) Operations, (4) Maintenance, and (5) Laboratory

and Test. Negroes were employed only in the Labor Department where the highest paying jobs paid less than the lowest paying jobs in the other four "operating" departments in which only whites were employed. ...

In 1955 the Company instituted a policy of requiring a high school education for initial assignment to any department except Labor and for transfer from the Coal Handling to any "inside" department (Operations, Maintenance, or Laboratory). When the Company abandoned its policy of restricting Negroes to the Labor Department in 1965, completion of high school also was made a prerequisite to transfer from Labor to any other department. From the time the high school requirement was instituted to the time of trial, however, white employees hired before the time of the high school education requirement continued to perform satisfactorily and achieve promotions in the "operating" departments.

The Company added a further requirement for new employees on July 2, 1965, the date on which Title VII became effective. To qualify for placement in any but the Labor Department it became necessary to register satisfactory scores on two professionally prepared aptitude tests, as well as to have a high school education. Completion of high school alone continued to render employees eligible for transfer to the four desirable departments from which Negroes had been excluded if the incumbent had been employed prior to the time of the new requirement. In September 1965 the Company began to permit incumbent employees who lacked a high school education to qualify for transfer from Labor or Coal Handling to an "inside" job by passing two tests - the

Wonderlic Personnel Test, which purports to measure general intelligence, and the Bennett Mechanical Comprehension Test. Neither was directed or intended to measure the ability to learn to perform a particular job or category of jobs. The requisite scores used for both initial hiring and transfer approximated the national median for high school graduates."[14]

The Court unanimously ruled: "What is required by Congress is the removal of artificial, arbitrary, and unnecessary barriers to employment when the barriers operate invidiously to discriminate on the basis of racial or other impermissible classification."[15] "What Congress has commanded is that any tests used must measure the person for the job and not the person in the abstract."[16] Subsequent legislation has now expressly regulated in 42 U.S.C. § 200e-2 (k) how disparate impact cases are analyzed. Subsection (k) (1) (A) (i) defines the basic approach in the disparate impact analysis as follows:

> An unlawful employment practice based on disparate impact is established under this subchapter only if—
>
> (i) a complaining party demonstrates that a respondent uses a particular employment practice that causes a disparate impact on the basis of race, color, religion, sex, or national origin and the respondent fails to demonstrate that the challenged practice is job related for the position in question and consistent with business necessity; ...

A plaintiff accordingly only has to demonstrate that a specific employment practice, such as requiring certain qualifications for a position, causes a statistical disparity between racial groups. The employer then has the burden of proof that the practice is related to the specific job in question.

Statistical disparities are relatively easy to show by simply comparing the demographic statistics in a geographic area to the numbers of individuals from a specific ethnic group hired for a specific type of job. Whether or not a particular employment practice or group of practices actually **causes** the disparity is a much more complex issue that can only be decided after a comprehensive review of the specific facts in a case. This entails lots of expensive work by lawyers and experts. The situation can be just as complex with the employer's defense that an employment practice is a business necessity. Employers mitigate the risk of expensive litigation by retaining experts, often lawyers who specialize in civil rights cases, to provide compliance advice on existing and planned employment practices.

Many companies and governmental agencies obtain permanent expertise by hiring "Chief Diversity Officers" at considerable expense. According to ZipRecruiter, the average salary for a "Diversity Inclusion Manager" in California was $ 129,467 as of 13 February 2023, compared to the national average of $ 129,798.[17] Salary.com states that the median salary in California for a Chief Diversity Officer is $ 263,400.[18] Be that as it may. Diversity managers cost a lot of money, especially after taking into account ancillary employment costs (e.g. employer contributions to Social Security, Medicare) as well as costs for office space, at least one administrative assistant, etc. Total annual costs could easily exceed $ 400,000.

There are also now countless DEI consulting firms that offer a wide range of services. These firms range from sole practitioners to large international consulting firms, such as McKinsey, that have established large DEI practices. There is also a wide range of costs. For example, NOVA, a mid-sized firm devoted solely to DEI consulting, states in general about DEI consulting costs, depending on the type of service:

- Single instructor-led training session: $500-$10,000

- Elearning modules: $200-$5,000

- Keynotes: $1,000 – $30,000[19]

The DEI consulting market was estimated to have had a volume of $ 3.4 billion in 2020 and is expected to at least double by 2027 with a compound annual growth rate ("CAGR") of 13%.[20] Harvard Kennedy School professor of public policy professor Iris Bohnet estimated in 2017 that approximately $ 8 billion was being spent annually on DEI training.[21] Regardless of the accurate number for DEI market volume, DEI consulting is now a booming industry involving lots of money.

There is a growing body of evidence that both gender diversity, as well as ethnic diversity in management and the workforce contribute to increased business performance. McKinsey % Co. found in 2017 that among the companies whose data were examined, the top quartile in terms of gender diversity was 21% more profitable than the lowest quartile and that the difference was even greater at 33% with regard to ethnic diversity.[22] The possible reasons for the correlation between diversity and profitability include having access to a larger talent pool, "enhanced decision making and depth of consumer insight, and strengthened employee engagement."[23]

However, the question about the benefits of diversity is completely different from the issue of whether or not DEI consulting and hiring DEI officers actually lead to more diversity. Professor Bohnet, after conducting extensive research, said in her interview in 2017, "Sadly enough, I did not find a single study that found that diversity training in fact leads to more diversity." Awkward, to say the least, that a multi-billion dollar industry cannot demonstrate any major success in achieving diversity.

There do not seem to be any studies yet about DEI services and their impact on diversity today, although there are anecdotal stories of success and failures. Clio Laboratories, a company based in Canada, reports some success in achieving diversity after implementing a program to increase the percentage of women engineers in their company. However, the key to success was discrimination: "To get there, we decided to use a quota, that's right, a quota."[24] Setting hiring quotas, i.e. affirmative action, is certainly an effective tool for increasing diversity. An organization that refuses to hire persons in the ethnic majority based on race or gender in order to increase the hiring of "marginalized" people from other races or another gender will, of course, increase diversity.

That might be permissible in Canada or other countries, but quotas are illegal in the United States under the Civil Rights Act of 1964 and related legislation. In the spring of 2022, two judges at the Superior Court in Los Angeles ruled that two California statutes that established quotas in boards of directors for women and "underrepresented" groups were unconstitutional because they violated the Equal Protection Clause in the California Constitution.[25]

Julie Diamond, an established executive consultant who has been in the field for more than 20 years and also provides DEI consulting, reports about the difficulties in achieving progress in diversity numbers in one case where management was willing and devoted considerable effort and expense to increase diversity in a financial services consulting company:

> The Director of HR, supported by the CEO and managing partners, called in a DEI consultant who surveyed female and minority employees and conducted exit interviews with ex-employees. ... [Various measures were implemented.] While this

increased the absolute number of female and Black employees, the rate of turnover and [personal improvement plans] didn't change, and promotions continued to lag. They were now 2 years into the process. **Frustrated to see such negligible results, they brought in another DEI consultant** who did more research and identified the key role that management played in supporting underrepresented employees. ... To address the ongoing problem, HR, together with the consultant, created obligatory inclusive management training for entry and mid-level managers. Nine months later, they looked at the data and saw a 4% increase in the number of Black employees, a 2% reduction in turnover, a slight increase in female partners ..., and no reduction in [personal improvement plans] for Black employees. **This lack of progress in DEI initiatives is not uncommon.**[26]
(Brackets and emphasis added)

The fact that DEI efforts often fail or are even counterproductive has been recognized even by supporters of DEI programs, although maintaining the view that DEI (and its jobs) will be needed indefinitely into the future.[27] Although corporations, driven by cost-benefit considerations, are now demonstrating their doubts about the effectiveness of DEI by cutting DEI staff,[28] not many authors have the courage to even question whether DEI programs and services make any sense. After all, bucking the trend in a multi-billion dollar industry does not make many friends, especially if the message is, "The Emperor has no clothes." In 2016, Frank Dobbin, head of the Department of Sociology at Harvard University, and Alexandra Kalev, chair of the Department of Sociology and Anthropology at Tel Aviv University, who authored the book *Getting to Diversity: What Works and What Doesn't*, wrote in a lengthy article:

It shouldn't be surprising that most diversity programs aren't increasing diversity. Despite a few new bells and whistles, courtesy of big data, companies are basically doubling down on the same approaches they've used since the 1960s—which often make things worse, not better. Firms have long relied on diversity training to reduce bias on the job, hiring tests and performance ratings to limit it in recruitment and promotions, and grievance systems to give employees a way to challenge managers. **Those tools are designed to preempt lawsuits by policing managers' thoughts and actions."** (emphasis added)

The numbers sum it up. Your organization will become less diverse, not more, if you require managers to go to diversity training, try to regulate their hiring and promotion decisions, and put in a legalistic grievance system. [29]

These authors have identified perhaps the main reason for the existence of DEI managers and DEI consulting. DEI managers and consulting firms serve as an "alibi". A company or governmental agency can preempt accusations of discrimination by demonstrating a proactive commitment to diversity, equity, and inclusion, especially by hiring a DEI manager and/or retaining DEI consulting services. The reputational benefits from demonstrably having a commitment to DEI are well recognized: "A public commitment to diversity helps position the organization as a desirable place to work."[30]

This "alibi" function was readily apparent after the death of George Floyd in May 2020. Kellie Wagner, the founder, and CEO of the DEI consulting firm Collective reportedly almost had to close her business after the COVID pandemic caused many of her clients to cancel her services for financial reasons. Her business and the DEI consulting industry, in general, started to boom again immediately after the death of George Floyd.

> Two days later [after moving from New York at the start of the rioting], Wagner was in Palm Springs — and her inbox was overrun with more than a hundred inquiries from prospective clients. Companies that had canceled on her two months prior were now desperate for help. There were a lot of white CEOs crying on the phone, Wagner recalls because they had crash-read Robin DiAngelo's *White Fragility* and were racked with guilt.
>
> Across the country, consultants in the diversity business felt that same whiplash of pandemic bust turning into a protest boom. Practitioners who were collecting unemployment received calls from the CEOs of major corporations looking to spend tens or hundreds of thousands of dollars publicly and fast.[31]

The alibi function results in pressure on corporations and governmental agencies to retain DEI consultants and hire DEI managers whether the expense is warranted or not. As is often the case when a problem is perceived, whether it exists or not, the first reaction is often, "We have to do something! Anything!" Senior management feels the imperative to act quickly so that they can announce something and show that they are proactive. Hiring a DEI consulting firm or employing a DEI manager are off-the-shelf actions that can be taken quickly and touted to critics. Whether or not DEI efforts will have any material results is a secondary concern. DEI efforts are difficult to measure and take a long time to show any success whatsoever. It's then hard to directly blame senior leadership for the lack of success because they can shift any blame to the DEI consultant or DEI director, and it is quite likely that at least some of the members in senior management in a company may have already changed employers or retired when the failure of DEI efforts is finally admitted.

Diversity, Equity & Inclusion consulting primarily deals with causes of statistical disparities in employment which do not rise to the level of violations of the law. Intentional or negligent violations of anti-discrimination laws, including violations revealed after a disparate effect analysis, are primarily matters for lawyers and cannot be litigated by DEI consultants before the courts. Unconscious bias is not *per se* illegal, although specific employment practices which result from unconscious bias might violate the law.[32] Even if no specific employment practices are identified which violate the law, unconscious bias can still affect employment statistics.

DEI consulting accordingly devotes considerable effort to the subject of unconscious bias. The Implicit Association Test ("IAT" – discussed above in Chapter IV) is one tool used to identify unconscious bias. Much of the work involves group training sessions with exercises such as "The Tag Game", the "Father-Son" activity, the "Circle of Trust",[33] "Café Society,"[34] and "Minute Mysteries.[35]" The descriptions for two of these exercises show why DEI consulting firms frequently fail to materially increase diversity:

> Murder Mysteries: "Romeo and Juliet are found dead lying on the floor in a pool of water. What happened? As with all Minute Mysteries, your group is then invited to ask a series of questions to solve the mystery of how Romeo and Juliet died. Spoiler Alert – I bet you immediately thought of the Shakespearean characters, right? Wrong. They are goldfish, and their tank broke, causing them to fall to the floor and die. The key here (your job) is to

transfer what your group learns from this (fictional) experience to the real world."[36]

Father-Son: "A father and son were involved in a car accident in which the father was killed, and the son was seriously injured. The father was pronounced dead at the scene of the accident, and his body was taken to a local morgue. The son was taken by ambulance to a nearby hospital and was immediately wheeled into an emergency operating room. A surgeon was called. Upon arrival and seeing the patient, the attending surgeon exclaimed, "Oh my God, it's my son!' Can you explain this?"

The probative value of these exercises in identifying unconscious bias is questionable. Virtually everyone in the United States or elsewhere in the English-speaking world knows Shakespeare's famous play about the ill-fated teenage lovers Romeo and Juliet and would accordingly associate their names to the characters in the play and not goldfish. The Father-Son exercise lives off the traditional impression, fostered over the course of decades by countless TV shows such as *Dr. Kildare* that a surgeon is normally a man and not a woman. Although perhaps a bit entertaining and possibly a welcome change for employees compared to their daily workload, these silly exercises are probably one reason why DEI training generally fails to achieve any material effects.

Strategies for controlling bias—which drive most diversity efforts—have failed spectacularly since they were introduced to promote equal opportunity. Black men have barely gained ground in corporate management since 1985. White women haven't progressed since 2000. It isn't that there aren't enough educated women and minorities out there—both groups have made huge educational gains over the past two generations. The problem is that we can't motivate people by forcing them to get with the program and punishing them if they don't.[37]

Many DEI directors and consultants are presumably frustrated and experiencing burnout due to their inability to achieve measurable success with their employers and clients. Some of this lies in the nature of the DEI industry. If success is actually achieved, it still takes a long time to show up in measurable data. Conscientious consultants and DEI officers often recognize that they are primarily acting as an alibi for senior management, and they may sense a lack of genuine support from management and possibly the entire organization.[38]

It is generally recognized that every person has some biases.[39] Unconscious "bias" may not even be a very accurate term. "Bias" is usually defined along the same line as prejudice, although the definition in Merriam-Webster is somewhat broader than "prejudice": "an inclination of temperament or outlook – especially: a personal and sometimes unreasoned judgment."[40] While "prejudice" necessarily involves rendering a judgment in advance of relevant knowledge, i.e. an "unreasoned judgment", "bias" sometimes is equivalent to "prejudice" and sometimes not. For example, the civil rights icon Jesse Jackson is well known for having said,

> There is nothing more painful to me at this stage in my life than to walk down the street and hear footsteps... then turn around and see somebody white and feel relieved.[41]

Perhaps Reverend Jackson's reaction is born of his experience on the streets of Chicago where there was and still is a lot of street crime committed by Blacks and relatively little committed by Whites, as indicated by arrest data showing e.g. 38,179 African Americans arrests in 2021 compared to 4,134 Whites (non-Hispanics) and 9,050

"White Hispanics."[42] Initial reactions based on past experience and knowledge are not biased or prejudiced and instead – especially in a potentially dangerous situation – represent a function of the survival instinct.

The word "bias" is pejorative. Do you or anyone you know in the United States or anywhere else want to be accused of being "biased"? However, there is no denying that individuals have personal preferences in countless areas, including aesthetics and physical attraction, as expressed in the title of the 1953 movie starring Marilyn Monroe *Gentlemen Prefer Blondes*. Is a member of an ethnic group prejudiced and a "racist" because that person feels more strongly attracted to members of the same ethnic group? Is a person a "racist" because they feel a stronger attraction to people of a different other ethnic group? Are we "racists" if we socialize mostly with people from one ethnic or cultural group?

Human beings have personal preferences which cannot be eliminated by force of law. There is also no need to do so or shame people for their personal preferences. The law does not and cannot regulate our feelings/preferences in our personal lives. The law instead regulates how we treat each other in our daily dealings at work, in school, etc. DEI consultants are well-advised to also focus on human interaction at the workplace and not on our personal feelings, i.e. personal preferences and unconscious biases, so long as personal feelings do not lead people to violate the law.

Companies, government agencies, and everyone concerned about unconscious bias must decide whether devoting billions of dollars and millions of hours to setting up DEI departments to fight unconscious bias makes sense and yields any material benefits for anyone other than the individuals employed in a DEI department. Many companies, including in the field of information technology,

have already reduced DEI staff.[43] Gov. Ron DeSantis of
Florida captured headlines when he signed Florida Senate
Bill No. 266 into law on May 15, 2023. That statute
expressly prohibits institutions in the Florida College
System from spending state or federal funds on "programs
or campus activities that: ... (b) Advocate for diversity,
equity, and inclusion, or promote or engage in political or
social activism as defined by rules of the State Board of
Education and regulations of the Board of Governors."[44]
This statute was adopted after Gov. DeSantis had requested
on December 28, 2022, that the Florida College System
report total DEI expenditures "of state resources on
programs and initiatives related to diversity, equity and
inclusion, and critical race theory within our state colleges
and universities."[45] The total expenditures are itemized in a
detailed spreadsheet in a total amount of approximately
$ 34.5 million.[46]

Big paydays

Any discussion about Critical Race Theory and money
would be remiss if it ignored some of the high fees and
royalties earned by CRT celebrities. For example, Robin
DiAngelo, the author of *White Fragility*, charges fees of
$ 30,000 to $ 40,000 when promoting the concepts of
"systemic racism" and CRT to corporations and other
audiences, in effect, selling dispensation.[47] Ibram X. Kendi
charged the University of Michigan $ 20,000 for a one-hour
virtual event.[48] He charged the same amount to the Fairfax
County school district in Virginia.[49] The inventor of the term
"intersectionality" Kimberlé Crenshaw, reportedly charges
$ 50,000 to $ 100,000 for a personal appearance.[50] Of
course, celebrities such as Robin DiAngelo and Ibram X
Kendi have every right to charge what the market will bear
when they find customers who are willing to pay. However,
it is *prima facie* fiscal malfeasance when public agencies

such as school districts or taxpayer-funded universities use taxpayer funds for events intended to be little more than a show. The term "race hustler" comes to mind.

Chapter Summary

Critical Race Theory has provided financial benefits for its proponents. The Black Lives Matter movement raised millions of dollars and has enabled the originators of the movement and their friends and relatives to profit personally as a result of lack of oversight. The people involved in the BLM movement have also demonstrated how quickly many supposed social justice warriors exploit the movement for personal gain and end up fighting over the spoils. Diversity, Equity & Inclusion consulting has become a multi-billion dollar business, and there are now also thousands of DEI directors throughout the private economy and especially in public agencies earning six-figure salaries. Any benefits from the massive expenditures for DEI throughout the economy are tenuous at best.

Much of the focus in DEI training is intended to address "unconscious (implicit) bias", something difficult to identify and which might be nothing more than individual preferences or, as is probably the case with Reverend Jesse Jackson, a reflection of past experience. The many billions of dollars spent on DEI efforts, especially the exorbitant fees paid to CRT celebrities, could certainly be spent for other purposes with much more benefit for businesses, schools, and governmental agencies.

---

[1]   Definition of "scam" in The Britannica Dictionary, https://www.britannica.com/dictionary/scam.

[2]   "About" tab at the BLMGNC website at https://blacklivesmatter.com/about/.

3   Maria Morava and Scottie Andrew, "The Black Lives Matter foundation raised $90 million in 2020, and gave almost a quarter of it to local chapters and organizations", CNN (February 25, 2021), https://www.cnn.com/2021/02/25/us/black-lives-matter-2020-donation-report-trnd/index.html.

4   Available as a pdf data file at https://blacklivesmatter.com/wp-content/uploads/2022/05/blmgnf-tc-form-990-2020-2021-01.pdf.

5   Ibid.

6   Andrew Buncombe, "Why did Black Lives Matter 'buy a $6m California Mansion'?", US edition of the Independent (April 6, 2022), available at https://www.independent.co.uk/news/world/americas/black-lives-matter-california-property-cullors-b2052447.html.

7   Isabel Vincent, "BLM's LA mansion sold for 250 percent more than the price of similar homes in the area", New York Post (April 6,2022), https://nypost.com/2022/04/06/blms-la-mansion-sold-for-250-times-the-price-of-other-homes-in-the-neighborhood/.

8   Stella Chan, "Black Lives Matter co-founder stepping down from organization", CNN (May 28, 2021), https://www.nytimes.com/2022/05/17/business/blm-black-lives-matter-finances.html

9   Available as a pdf data file at https://blacklivesmatter.com/wp-content/uploads/2022/09/audit-report-blmgnf-fy2021.pdf.

10   IRS Form 990 for BLMGNF, (see footnote 4), at pg. 8.

11   Ibid.

12   Open Letter available at https://form.jotform.com/222483990775166.

13   Black Lives Matter Grassroots, Inc. vs. Black Lives Matter Global Network Foundation, Inc., case no. 228TCV28481, August 31, 2022, pdf copy available at https://www.scribd.com/document/591075168/Black-Lives-Matter-Grassroots-v-BLMGNF#.

14   *Griggs v. Duke Power Co., 401 U.S. 424 (1971)* at pp. 427, 428, https://tile.loc.gov/storage-services/service/ll/usrep/usrep401/usrep401424/usrep401424.pdf

15   Ibid., pg. 431.

16   Ibid., pg. 436.

17   Published on ZipRecruiter, https://www.ziprecruiter.com/Salaries/Diversity-Inclusion-Manager-

Salary--in-
California#:~:text=As%20of%20Feb%2012%2C%202023,be%20appro
ximately%20%2462.24%20an%20hour (accessed on April 14, 2023).

[18] Salary.com at
https://www.salary.com/research/salary/alternate/chief-diversity-
officer-salary/ca, (accessed on April 14, 2023).

[19.] "What's The Cost Of Diversity, Equity, and Inclusion?", The
Nova Collective, https://www.thenovacollective.com/who-we-
are/#about, (accessed on 21 February 2023).

[20.] Summary of a report "Global Diversity and Inclusion (D&I)
Industry" (October 2022), in ReportLinker,
https://www.reportlinker.com/p06219616/Global-Diversity-and-
Inclusion-D-I-Industry.html?utm_source=GNW.

[21] Interview with Iris Bohnet. "Focusing on what works for
workplace diversity", McKinsey and Company (April 7, 2917),
https://www.mckinsey.com/featured-insights/gender-equality/focusing-
on-what-works-for-workplace-diversity.

[22] Vivian Hunt, Sara Prince, Sundiatu Dixon-Fyle, Lareina Yee,
"Delivering through Diversity", McKinsey & Co. (January 2018), pg.
8,
https://www.mckinsey.com/~/media/mckinsey/business%20functions/p
eople%20and%20organizational%20performance/our%20insights/deliv
ering%20through%20diversity/delivering-through-diversity_full-
report.pdf.

[23] Ibid., pg. 5.

[24] Ainsley Robinson, "How we doubled the representation of
women in Engineering at Clio", Clio Labs (August 28, 2019),
https://labs.clio.com/how-we-doubled-the-representation-of-women-in-
engineering-at-clio-2d9a4a1a0282.

[25] Alec Shemmel, "California court upholds ban on race, gender
quotas for corporate boards", Fox26News (December 20, 2023),
https://kmph.com/news/local/california-court-upholds-ban-on-race-
gender-quotas-for-corporate-boards.

[26] Patrick Kitchen, "DEI Data: Understanding the What and the
Why", online at diamond leadership (December 27, 2021),
https://diamondleadership.com/articles/dei-data/.

[27] "Are Workplace Diversity Programs Doing More Harm Than
Good", The New York Times – The Argument panel discussion
(August 11, 2021) at

https://www.nytimes.com/2021/08/11/opinion/workplace-diversity-dei-initiative.html?showTranscript=1.

[28]   Reyhan Ayas, Paulina Aceves, Devan Rawlings, "Cutting Costs at the Expense of Diversity", revelio labs (February 7, 2023), at https://www.reveliolabs.com/news/social/cutting-costs-at-the-expense-of-diversity/.

[29]   Frank Dobbin and Alexandra Kalev, "Why Diversity Programs Fail", Harvard Business Review (July-August 2016), available at https://hbr.org/2016/07/why-diversity-programs-fail.

[30]   Marie Y. Phillipe, "Diversity Power in the Corporate Image", in Profiles of Diversity Journal (August 31, 2011), https://diversityjournal.com/5695-diversity-power-in-the-corporate-image/.

[31].   Bridget Read, ""Doing the Work at Work: What are companies desperate for diversity consultants actually buying?", in The Cut (May 26, 2021), https://www.thecut.com/article/diversity-equity-inclusion-industrial-companies.html.

[32]   "Is Unconscious Bias In The Workplace Illegal?" published online at the website of the Pennsylvania law firm Ruppert Manes Narahari at https://lawkm.com/is-unconscious-bias-in-the-workplace-illegal/.

[33]   These exercises are described in " 'A-Ha' Activities for Unconscious Bias Training" on the website of Culture Plus Consulting, an Australian DEI consulting firm, https://cultureplusconsulting.com/2018/08/16/a-ha-activities-for-unconscious-bias-training/.

[34]   Café Society is described in "Implicit Bias Training Exercises: What You Should Know" on the website of the consulting firm Impactly, Inc., https://www.getimpactly.com/post/implicit-bias-training-exercises.

[35]   Minute Mysteries is described in "4+ Activities to Explore Unconscious Bias" on the website of playmeo.pty.ltd., https://www.playmeo.com/4-activities-to-explore-unconscious-bias/.

[36]   Ibid.

[37]   Frank Dobbin and Alexandra Kalev, "Why Diversity Programs Fail", in Harvard Business Review (July-August 2016), https://hbr.org/2016/07/why-diversity-programs-fail.

[38]   Arthur Woods, "Why Many DEI Leaders Are Experiencing Burnout and How you Can Fix It", in Inc.com (April 15, 2022),

https://www.inc.com/arthur-woods/why-many-dei-leaders-are-experiencing-burnout-how-you-can-fix-it.html.

39   Karen Steinhauser, "Everyone Is a Little Bit Biased"; Business Law Section of the American Bar Association" (March 16, 2020), https://www.americanbar.org/groups/business_law/publications/blt/2020/04/everyone-is-biased/.

40   Definition 1a for "Bias" in Merriam Webster Dictionary online, https://www.merriam-webster.com/dictionary/bias.

41   Quoted from "goodreads.com", https://www.goodreads.com/quotes/5978-there-is-nothing-more-painful-to-me-at-this-stage.

42   20212 Annual Report, Chicago Police Department, pg. 102, at https://home.chicagopolice.org/wp-content/uploads/2021-Annual-Report.pdf#page=101&zoom=100,0,0.

43   Kelsey Butler, "Big Tech Layoffs Are Hitting Diversity and Inclusion Jobs Hard" (January 24, 2023), https://www.bloomberg.com/news/articles/2023-01-24/tech-layoffs-are-hitting-diversity-and-inclusion-jobs-hard#xj4y7vzkg.

44   Florida Senate Bill No. 266, Section 4 1004.06 (2) (b), at https://laws.flrules.org/2023/82.

45   Office of the Governor, Memo # 23-021 (December 28, 2022), at https://twitter.com/BryanDGriffin/status/1610710708135821312/photo/1.

46   Available at https://drive.google.com/file/d/1vQbcRDZmWzewqD_vuFx97zjTIscoG1O8/view.

47   Robin DiAngelo's "Keynote Speaker Fee" is $30,00 - $40,000, https://www.bigspeak.com/speakers/diangelo-r/ (accessed on April 16, 2023).

48   Mckenna Dallmeyer and Adam Sabes, " EXCLUSIVE: UMich paid Kendi $20k for a one-hour virtual event", in Campus Reform (October 14, 2021), https://www.campusreform.org/article?id=18308.

49   Asra Q Nomani and Heather Zwicker, "County residents raise questions about contracts with sources who argue for 'new discriminations' and 'unequal' protocols, as school superintendent admits to problems with 'internal practices' ", Fairfax County Times (January 8, 2023, updated on January 12, 2023), https://www.fairfaxtimes.com/articles/fairfax_county/county-residents-

raise-questions-about-contracts-with-sources-who-argue-for-new-discriminations-and-unequal/article_c8b18298-9068-11ed-ae18-3fe5457eb040.html.

[50]   Jeremiah Poff, "Law professor who designed critical race theory charges $100K for lectures: Report", Washington Examiner (January 24, 2023), https://www.washingtonexaminer.com/policy/education/crt-law-professor-charges-100k-for-lectures-report.

Chapter VII

The Goals

An ideology such as Critical Race Theory has social and political goals and constitutes the philosophical basis for a political movement with specific goals. An ideology based on dialectic that divides society into the oppressor class and the oppressed necessarily develops an "us versus them" approach as the starting point for political action. The proponents of the ideology accordingly need an enemy, be it the bourgeoisie or "white supremacy." A strong emotional appeal is the next ingredient in transforming the ideology into a large-scale political reality.

Identifying a real enemy or just pasting the label of "enemy" on a group and then appealing to base emotions of hate, fear, and envy has been a favorite strategy of tyrants throughout history. How better to gain and hold political power and concomitant wealth and prestige than by whipping up emotional fervor against a real or perceived enemy? The only major downside risk for the dictators is if the strategy leads to conflict with a real enemy and that enemy wins. In that case, the greater the enemy's victory, the greater the loss of power and wealth. Defeated dictators may even lose their lives, as the world witnessed many times in just the 20th century.

The proponents of Critical Race Theory readily admit that CRT is not just an academic exercise and instead also constitutes a political and social movement.

> CRT was not, however, simply a product of a philosophical critique of the dominant frames on racial power. It was also a product of activists' engagement with the material manifestations of liberal reform. Indeed, one might say that CRT was the offspring of a post-civil rights institutional

activism that was generated and informed by an oppositionalist orientation toward racial power.[1]

George Lipsitz, Professor of Black Studies and Sociology at the University of California in Santa Barbara, writing in praise of Kimberlé Crenshaw and her representation of CRT, writes:

> The social movement history of CRT tells us that struggle is generative and productive, that organizational learning changes both people and social structures, that deliberative talk and face-to-face decision-making make a difference. Yet it is often difficult for academics to imagine themselves as activists. We are more comfortable with ideas, evidence, arguments, and opinions than with action. The relentless segregation of society systematically separates us from the social groups with whom we most need to be in touch. Yet all across this nation and all across this world, people are standing up and stepping up and speaking up.[2]

Rejection of "Whiteness" and Assimilation

Critical Race Theory makes no bones about who and what the "enemy" is: "Whiteness" is the overarching term for everything CRT opposes. Whether called "systemic racism," "white supremacy," or "unconscious bias," the concept of "whiteness" in CRT actually refers to American society in general.

> Whiteness and white racialized identity refer to the way that white people, their customs, culture, and beliefs operate as the standard by which all other groups of [sic] are compared. Whiteness is also at the core of understanding race in America. Whiteness and the normalization of white racial identity throughout America's history have created a culture

where nonwhite persons are seen as inferior or abnormal.

This white-dominant culture also operates as a social mechanism that grants advantages to white people, since they can navigate society both by feeling normal and being viewed as normal Persons who identify as white rarely have to think about their racial identity because they live within a culture where whiteness has been normalized.

Whiteness (and its accepted normality) also exist as everyday microaggressions toward people of color. Acts of microaggressions include verbal, nonverbal, and environmental slights, snubs or insults toward nonwhites. Whether intentional or not, these attitudes communicate hostile, derogatory, or harmful messages.[3]

"Whiteness" is understood by the proponents of CRT to be virtually everything in modern American society and culture, as is readily apparent from the now infamous "Whiteness Chart" published online in 2020 by the National Museum of African American History & Culture (NMAAHC"), a division of the Smithsonian Institution.[4] The characteristics attributed to "White Culture" in that truly bizarre chart include:

- Rugged Individualism – The individual is the primary unit – self-reliance,

- Family structure – The nuclear family: father. Mother. 2.3 children is the ideal social unit

- Emphasis on the Scientific Method – Objective, rational linear thinking, Cause and effect relationships, Quantitative emphasis

- History – Based on Northern European Immigrants' experience in the United States, ... The primacy of Western (Greek, Roman) and Judeo-Christian tradition

- Protestant Work Ethic – Hard work is the key to success, Work before play...

- Religion – Christianity is the norm, ... No tolerance for deviation from single god concept

- Status, Power & Authority ... Respect authority, Heavy value on ownership of goods, space, property,

- Future orientation – Plan for future ...

- Time – Follow rigid time schedules, ...

Images of the chart can easily be found by searching for "Whiteness chart" on Google. The NMAAHC pulled the chart off its site a short time after it was published due to heavy criticism.[5] However, the chart still shows how the people at the NMAAHC view "whiteness" because the chart obviously took time and effort to produce and was presumably a collaborative piece of work that was carefully vetted by higher-ups at the NMAAHC before posting it online.

The Whiteness Chart and similar efforts to "deconstruct whiteness" are blatantly racist against Whites but also against "people of color" because this absurd material implies that "people of color" cannot "Plan for the future," "Follow rigid time schedules," and apply the scientific method. This attitude is also reflected by leading academicians in the field of Critical Race Theory. Delgado and Stefancic write in the leading textbook on Critical Race Theory that meritocracy, rational thinking, the scientific method, and a hard work ethic are racist.[6]

Critical Race Theory and its followers are adept at exploiting emotion to achieve their purpose. CRT expressly nurtures the tool of "storytelling" to further the cause (discussed above in Chapter IV point 7). Whether the story is true or not is irrelevant. The main purpose of storytelling is to achieve emotional impact. In recent years, storytelling triggered riots, such as in Ferguson, Missouri, after Michael Brown was killed in 2014, and especially during the summer of 2020 when riots erupted in several major cities, and demonstrations took place throughout the country.

The language used by organizations such as BLM is aggressive and recalls the Marxist revolutionary fervor of the late 1960s. The jargon in the CRT movement talks about "resistance" and "struggle" and accordingly benefits from favorable connotations linked to these terms from completely different contexts, such as *La Résistance* in France during World War II. Anyone who doubts that "resistance" has favorable connotations need only listen to the "La resistance" medley in the 1999 animated film "South Park: Bigger, Longer & Uncut".[7]

The efforts by the proponents of Critical Race Theory initially in a few law schools have resulted in the racist, hateful ideology of CRT that has spread like a virus throughout academia and is now making headway throughout American society. A recent Rasmussen poll[8] conducted in February 2023 asked whether people agreed with the statement, "It's OK to be white" and whether they agreed with a second statement, "Black people can be racist, too." Although a relatively large majority of all persons polled, both black and white, agreed with the statements, it is disturbing that 26% of black respondents answered the first question with "No" and another 21% said they were not sure.

194 THE CRITICAL RACE THEORY $CAM

The ultimate goals of Critical Race Theory go far beyond the "equity" of lower standards or even reparations. CRT is directed towards a complete transformation of American society into a collectivist nightmare in which people are classified according to race. Individual advancement would then depend more on pedigree and less on individual merit. This is clearly expressed by leading voices in the CRT movement. Delgado and Stefancic write,

> Only aggressive, color-conscious efforts to change the way things are will do much to ameliorate misery.[9]

Ibram X. Kendi is much more blunt in his best-seller *How to be an Antiracist* when he calls for perpetual racial discrimination:

> The only remedy to stop racist discrimination is antiracist discrimination. The only remedy to past discrimination is present discrimination. The only remedy to present discrimination is future discrimination.[10]

The "melting pot" became a popular term for describing the United States, especially after the play "The Melting Pot" used the term in 1908 as a metaphor for people from different nations, cultures, and ethnicities learning to live together and assimilating into the American culture.[11] Kendi completely trashes the idea of a society in which people adapt to certain common standards as a reasonable basis for getting along when he writes, "Assimilationist ideas are racist ideas."[12]

Rejection of capitalism

The Critical Race Theory ideology opposes free market capitalism, the economic system that defeated Marxism and has undisputedly resulted in a higher standard of living for billions of people throughout the world than could ever have been imagined 100 years ago. Critical Race Theory's rejection of capitalism is a direct consequence of CRT's philosophical roots in Marxism and the dialectic approach. Even prior to the emergence of CRT in the 1970s and 1980s, many leaders in the black nationalist movement and also the broader civil rights movement opposed capitalism. Angela Davis studied for her bachelor's degree with Herbert Marcuse at Brandeis University and continued her graduate work at the resurrected Frankfurt School before earning her doctorate at the Humboldt University in East Berlin. She then returned to the United States and became a member of the Communist Party.[13] Angela Davis is attributed with the quote, "Racism cannot be separated from capitalism."[14] She maintains that position in a 2021 interview online: "We can't eradicate racism without eradicating capitalism."[15] Malcolm X was also certainly no friend of capitalism:

> You can't operate a capitalistic system unless you are vulturistic; you have to have someone else's blood to suck to be a capitalist. You show me a capitalist, I'll show you a bloodsucker. He cannot be anything but a bloodsucker if he's going to be a capitalist.[16]

Martin Luther King also had a critical view of capitalism, apparently based in large part on his training as a Baptist minister and possibly a lack of knowledge about free market economics. He questioned capitalism as early as 1952 at the age of 23 in a letter to Coretta Scott, who he married one year later. His opposition to capitalism became more pronounced as he saw that the 1960s civil rights legislation had not immediately resulted in material, economic benefit for Blacks.

> We have moved from the era of civil rights to the era of human rights, an era where we are called upon to raise certain basic questions about the whole society. We have been in a reform movement... But after

> Selma and the voting rights bill, we moved into a new era, which must be the era of revolution. We must recognize that we can't solve our problem now until there is a radical redistribution of economic and political power... this means a revolution of values and other things. We must see now that the evils of racism, economic exploitation and militarism are all tied together... you can't really get rid of one without getting rid of the others... the whole structure of American life must be changed. America is a hypocritical nation and [we] must put [our] own house in order.[17]

The fundamental premise in CRT, according to which racism is the normal way society conducts business (see Chapter IV point 1), is reflected in the concept of "racial capitalism – the process of deriving social or economic value from the racial identity of another person."[18] Capitalism and racism are both described as forms of exploitation for profit inherently linked with each other.[19] Ibram X. Kendi succinctly writes:

> To love capitalism is to end up loving racism. To love racism is to end up loving capitalism. The conjoined twins are two sides of the same destructive body.[20]

Kendi goes even beyond calling for the elimination of capitalism in order to cleanse American society of racism. He has proposed amending the U.S. Constitution to create a "Department of Antiracism" that would be able to exercise totalitarian control over all American society:

> To fix the original sin of racism, Americans should pass an anti-racist amendment to the U.S. Constitution that enshrines two guiding anti-racist principals [sic]: Racial inequity is evidence of racist policy and the different racial groups are equals. The

amendment would make unconstitutional racial inequity over a certain threshold, as well as racist ideas by public officials (with "racist ideas" and "public official" clearly defined). It would establish and permanently fund the Department of Anti-racism (DOA) comprised of formally trained experts on racism and no political appointees. The DOA would be responsible for preclearing all local, state and federal public policies to ensure they won't yield racial inequity, monitor those policies, investigate private racist policies when racial inequity surfaces, and monitor public officials for expressions of racist ideas. The DOA would be empowered with disciplinary tools to wield over and against policymakers and public officials who do not voluntarily change their racist policy and ideas.[21]

This idea is so absurd that it raises doubts about whether Kendi was serious when proposing such a "supra-department" with authority over every policy and official in the United States, a proposal completely contrary to the fundamental concepts of federalism and limited authority of the federal government. Perhaps he chose the acronym "DOA" in full knowledge of the traditional meaning "dead on arrival." If Kendi is serious, however, he may perhaps want to serve as the first Secretary of the Department of Anti-racism, a position he would equip with dictatorial power.

Chapter Summary

Critical Race Theory, just like its precursor ideology Marxism, is directed toward a revolutionary transformation of the United States into a country with a socialist economy in which individuals advance primarily on the basis of their racial identity. As has been the case in all socialist experiments, power would lie in the hands of people in an ideologically elite class. Individualism and merit would play, at best, only a subordinate role. The proponents of CRT are already hard at work eliminating and lowering performance standards in the name of "equity," and the efforts to dumb down American society continue. The blatant racism (in the traditional sense of the term) shown by over one-quarter of the black respondents in recent polling suggests that Critical Race Theory is having substantial success with its condemnation of "whiteness." If CRT achieves its ultimate goal of fundamentally transforming the United States, the American people will be condemned to living in a totalitarian, socialist nation dominated by racists (in the traditional sense of the term).

-----

[1]   Kimberlé Crenshaw, "Twenty Years of Critical Race Theory: Looking Backward To Move Forward", Connecticut Law Review, volume 43 no. 5 (July 2011), pp. 1253-1352 at pg. 1260, https://opencommons.uconn.edu/cgi/viewcontent.cgi?article=1116&context=law_review.

[2]   George Lipsitz, "Critical Race Theory as a Social Movement!", Connecticut Law Review, volume 43 no. 5 (July 2011), pp. 1459-1478 at pg. 1478, https://core.ac.uk/download/pdf/302394504.pdf.

[3]   "Talking About Race - Whiteness", National Museum of African American History & Culture, division of the Smithsonian Institution, https://nmaahc.si.edu/learn/talking-about-race/topics/whiteness (accessed on April 16, 2023).

[4]   Valerie Richardson, " African American museum removes 'whiteness' chart over claims of backhanded racism", The Washington Times (July 17, 2020), https://www.washingtontimes.com/news/2020/jul/17/smithsonian-african-american-museum-remove-whitene/

[5]   Ibid.

[6]   Delgado/Stefancic, pp. 132 et seq.

[7]   South Park song "La resistance", https://www.youtube.com/watch?v=LonKGuS9uuQ.

[8]   Paul Bedard, " 'It's OK to be white,' agree 72/, including 53/ of black people," Washington Examiner, (February 22, 2023), at https://www.washingtonexaminer.com/news/washington-secrets/its-ok-to-be-white-agree-72-including-53-of-blacks.

[9]   Delgado/Stefancic, pg. 27.

[10]   Ibram C. Kendi, *How to be an Antiracist*, pg. 31.

[11]   Wikipedia article on "Melting Pot," at https://en.wikipedia.org/wiki/Melting_pot.

[12]   Ibid. pg. 51.

[13]   Faculty member biography of Angela Davis as Professor at the European Graduate School, https://egs.edu/biography/angela-davis/ (accessed on April 16, 2023).

[14]   Turtle Quotes, "31 Angela Davis Quotes On Race, Feminism & More" (May 1, 2022), https://turtlequote.com/angela-davis-quotes/.

[15]   Interview with "Democracy Now!" on YouTube, https://www.youtube.com/watch?v=qhh3CMkngkY.

[16]   Malcolm X speech at the Audubon Ballroom on December 20, 1964, text available at https://teachingamericanhistory.org/document/at-the-audubon/.

[17]   Dr. Martin Luther King, Jr., report to the staff of the Southern Christian Leadership Conference in May 1967 quoted as item 2 in "Quotations from Rev. Dr. Martin Luther King, Jr." compiled by the Poverty Initiative at Union Theological Seminary, https://kairoscenter.org/wp-content/uploads/2014/11/King-quotes-2-page.pdf.

[18]   Nancy Leong, "Racial Capitalism", Harvard Law Review, volume 125 issue 8 (June 2013), pp. 2151-2226, at 2153, https://harvardlawreview.org/print/vol-126/racial-capitalism/.

[19]   Edna Bonacich, "Racism in Advanced Capitalist Society: Comments on William J. Wilson's The Truly Disadvantaged," The Journal of Sociology & Social Welfare: Vol. 16 : issue 4 , Article 4 (1989). https://scholarworks.wmich.edu/jssw/vol16/iss4/4.

[20]   Ibram C. Kendi, *How to be an Antiracist*, pg. 301.

[21]   Ibram X. Kendi, "Pass an Anti-Racist Constitutional Amendment", in Politico, https://www.politico.com/interactives/2019/how-to-fix-politics-in-america/inequality/pass-an-anti-racist-constitutional-amendment/ (accessed on April 16, 2023).

Chapter VIII

Resist

The by far greatest ideological conflict in the United States and increasingly other Western countries such as Great Britain is between Critical Race Theory and the concept of equal protection under the law for all individuals embodied in the 14th Amendment and reflected by Dr. Martin Luther King, Jr. in his "I have a Dream" speech in 1963. Equal protection is a fundamental principle for any legal system based on the rule of law. The Civil Rights Movement finally achieved the goal of equal protection for everyone when the Civil Rights Bill of 1964 and subsequent civil rights legislation were passed. Critical Race Theory is dedicated to returning to a society with a caste system based on ethnic pedigree. Nobody in their right mind could possibly want to live in such a society. Unless you wish to live under the constant, totalitarian rule of racism (in the traditional sense of the term), the only alternative is *la résistance*! The recently published book *The Great Parent Revolt - How Parents and Grassroots Leaders Are Fighting Critical Race Theory in America's Schools* by Lance Izumi, Wenyuan Wu, and McKenzie Richards is an excellent selection of cases of practical resistance, including litigation.

Knowledge and courage

This chapter discusses various steps we can all take to shrink Critical Race Theory back down to where it started as a sideshow in academia. It deserves study and expenditure of resources at most only to the same extent our educational institutions teach about the defeated ideologies of communism and fascism. You have already taken the first step if you have read this far. Namely, you now know what Critical Race Theory is and how it functions. It's simply not possible to effectively challenge CRT unless you know what you're talking about.

The second step is to learn to identify instances of practical implementation of CRT in your local community and especially your schools. It is not always easy to recognize when a policy is based on CRT. For example, a community might have a "diversity council" or "diversity commission." That is not by itself a matter of concern. The actions taken by such a committee, however, might cross the line.

Any action that smacks of racism (in the traditional sense of the term), such as giving preferential consideration to job applicants of one race compared to others, is highly suspect and, of course, also illegal. Any lowering of hiring standards based on the argument that a higher, reasonable standard leads to racial disparities is a policy based on CRT. Any change in criminal law and prosecution based on the argument that the statute in question or the level of prosecution leads to racial disparities is the result of CRT. In general, you should be suspicious of any policy that is supported by the argument that it will increase "equity" or is necessary to reduce a socio-economic disparity between ethnic groups. The policy still might be acceptable, depending on whether the policy distinguishes according to race, but in any event, the policy deserves careful scrutiny.

Once you know what CRT is and are able to recognize it in practice, the third step is mustering up the courage to publicly oppose actions based on CRT. Opposing CRT invariably results in animosity on the part of some people. Be prepared to be called "Racist!" A defensive mode in response to such an accusation (e.g. "I am not. Some of my best friends are [*ethnic designation*]") is weak and plays into the hands of the person hurling the insult; personal attacks are a long recognized tool intended to draw an opponent off-topic. A better response is roughly as follows: "It seems that all you can do is throw baseless insults rather than engage in a reasonable discussion. Any further discussion with you is a waste of time until you return to civil discourse." You simply have to develop a thick skin when opposing CRT because you will be met with hostility. After all, you are not just intellectually challenging people. In many situations, your opposition to CRT by, for example, questioning a school district's expenditure for DEI consulting, can cost a lot of money to people who have made a business out of selling CRT snake oil.

Now that you are armed with knowledge about the theory and practice of Critical Race and are willing to "join battle with the enemy", what practical steps can you take. The "battle" is, of course, in reality, a debate, and the "enemy" are the supporters of CRT based policies who may well be well-meaning but uninformed family members, friends, neighbors, colleagues at work, etc. Your "weapon" is knowledgeable, civil discourse directed towards educating others about CRT and why you oppose it. Feel free to engage in discussion with others who express positions in support of CRT so long as the discussion remains civil. Make use of the opportunity for public comment at school board meetings and city council meetings when CRT-related issues come up. Now for some practical pointers:

Getting and analyzing specific information

Make full use of your rights under **freedom of information laws**. For example, if your school district or local community has contracted for DEI services, ask that the terms of the contract and the instructional materials be disclosed, preferably before the contract is awarded. Many DEI consultants refuse to allow disclosure of their course materials based on the argument that the materials are intellectual property and protected by copyright. The simple rule in such a situation should always be, "No disclosure, no contract." If a contract has already been issued, there might still be possibilities to obtain disclosure under freedom of information laws based on the argument that a public agency cannot avoid public disclosure of information by using a private company to fulfill a task that the agency is authorized to perform. It is also possible that an employee forced to participate in DEI training sessions might disclose materials despite being told to keep them confidential.

You can always check your children's school materials and bring a book or other material to the attention of the school and district administration when you find something objectionable. You must be able to show how a book, for example, contains CRT propaganda and why specific points are objectionable. I was recently (February 2023) asked to look into a situation in which an elementary school district in the San Francisco Bay Area had distributed a link to parents for the video reading of the book *Our Skin – A First Conversation about Race* (https://video.link/w/4uFUc) by Megan Madison, Jessica Balli, and Isabel Roxas. The book is harmless until page 18, up to that point with an accurate discussion of the obvious fact that people can have different skin colors and that skin color does not say anything about who a person is, all accompanied by pleasant, colorful pictures of children. Then comes page 18 with a dark and dismal picture of skulls under glass and the text:

> A long time ago, before you were born, a group of white people made up an idea called race. They sorted people by skin color and said that white people were better, smarter, prettier and that they deserve more than everybody else.

This statement fits well under the banner of CRT because it uses storytelling to raise a general accusation against "a group of white people". The accusation is also consistent with the concept of "race as a social construct". As is often the case, the accusation is factually wrong. The National Museum of African American History and Culture traces the word "race" back to the 1500s, well before the first British settlers arrived in Jamestown (1607) and also well before the year 1619.[1] The accusation also ignores the etymology of the word "race" which traces the term in the sense of "people of common descent" past the 1500s back to Middle English and possibly even further back to Arabic (*ra's*) and Hebrew (*rosh*).[2] As with all modern words, meanings have evolved over time, and the same word can have completely different meanings. The noun "race" can also mean an athletic competition or a creek.

Our Skin has a further weakness common in many "CRT-informed" works; it is extremely Eurocentric and makes no mention of racism in any other part of the world. Contrary to this myopic approach, the lead sentence in the Wikipedia entry for "Racism in Asia" reads: "Racism in Asia has roots in events that have happened from thousands of years ago to the present." The entry then embarks on an examination of racism in various Asian countries. A recent article published in the Asian online publication "The Diplomat" is titled "Asia Has Its Own Strands of Racism. It's Time to Take Them Seriously" and has the interesting subtitle, "Racism is a problem around the world, but is often overlooked when the problem doesn't fit neatly into the much-discussed American framework."[3]

Perhaps the most disturbing aspect of the book *Our Skin* is how it introduces the concept of racism on pages 20 and 21 by showing three laughing white kids running up a flight of stairs ahead of a protesting black child who is being held back from even getting on the stairs by an officious looking white man. The text on page 20 reads, "When people believe this untrue story about race, that's called racism." The text on pg. 21 reads:

> Racism is also the things people do and the unfair rules they make about race so that white people get

more power, and are treated better, than everybody else. Racism happens in lots of big and small ways. It's all around us, even if we don't often notice it.

This is consistent with two aspects of CRT. First, racism is stated to be something that only "white people" engage in, one of the odd teachings derived from the redefinition of "racism" to mean "racial prejudice + power." Second, the last quoted sentence restates the primary tenet of Critical Race Theory, according to which racism is the "normal way we do business." Especially in the case of little children who already have a basic understanding of fairness, this imagery and language can obviously create the impression that all white people are racists and unfair. This can, in turn, potentially result in race-based violence. The possibility of children engaging in racially motivated violence is not a paranoid fear: News Channel 8 in Tampa, Florida, reported with The Associated Press on March 11, 2022:

> COCONUT CREEK, Fla. (AP) — Five Florida middle schoolers are facing battery and hate crime charges after police said they attacked white students using racial taunts and slurs.
>
> Coconut Creek police said four white children between the ages of 11 and 12 years old were assaulted Wednesday by the group that yelled things like "it's opposite day" and "brown power."
>
> The attacks happened at a community center where children gather before the first bell at Lyons Creek Middle School, according to police reports.
>
> The charges filed were misdemeanors, although the hate crime allegation could trigger a felony count depending on decisions by prosecutors. Coconut Creek is a suburb of Fort Lauderdale.[4]

Racial tension and resulting violence can hurt all children, both the victims and the perpetrators. School administrators should consider, in any event, the potential civil liability if they use material engendering racial tension and a violent incident subsequently occurs.

Legislation and resolutions banning the teaching of CRT in public schools

Schools with grades K-12 are now a major battlefield in the fight against the racist ideology of Critical Race Theory. Many states have adopted or are considering legislation that prohibits teaching Critical Race Theory in grades K-12 and also in other institutions. Florida's legislation was the reason why Governor DeSantis and the Florida Department of Education rejected a proposed advanced placement (AP) African-American history course curriculum established by the College Board.[5]

As mentioned in the Introduction, the author of this book drafted the resolution adopted in August 2021 that banned teaching CRT in the Paso Robles Joint Unified School District ("PRJUSD") in California. That resolution, as well as an earlier resolution condemning racism, passed in March 2021 at the same time the school district approved a "constructive" ethnic studies course, have resolved or at least calmed down race-related issues that many other school districts are currently facing. Our Paso Robles experience may serve as a guide for action in other school districts.

George Floyd's death in May 2020 continued to occupy the country well into the beginning of 2021. Diversity councils and committees were established in countless communities and institutions. School districts throughout California started adopting "Anti-racism Resolutions" at the end of 2020 and the early part of 2021. The diversity council in Paso Robles asked the administration of the PRJUSD to submit such a resolution to the school board for adoption. I was president of the school board at the time. Our administration prepared a draft by copying and pasting from resolutions that had been adopted in other school districts; our administration told us that the draft had then been toned down compared to resolutions in other districts. I took one look at the draft and rejected it outright because it was based on Critical Race Theory and, in effect, was a *mea culpa* for white Americans. Instead, I drafted a "Resolution Condemning Racism" (copy attached as **Appendix I**), which started with Dr. Martin Luther King's famous quote about judging people by the content of their character and not the color of their skin. The basic message was that the PRJUSD does not tolerate any racism by anyone whatsoever.

At the same time, many students at Paso Robles High School were requesting that an ethnic studies course be established. The high school had actually had such a course almost ten years earlier in the form of a history course until the teacher retired. One of our teachers Mr. Land, who can accurately be described as favoring the political left and possibly even as an activist but who is also an excellent teacher, prepared a draft curriculum modeled to a great extent on the standard curriculum that had been recently adopted by California as the basis for the ethnic studies course that will become a requirement for graduation from high school in a few years. Aside from insisting that the word "Latinx" be struck from the curriculum because that term is neither proper English nor proper Spanish, I set three basic conditions for my support of the course:

- The course could not be based on Critical Race Theory, as is the case with so-called "liberated" ethnic studies courses. Instead, the course would have to be structured as an accurate history course that dealt with various ethnic groups that now make up American society, i.e. a "constructive" ethnic studies course.

- The course could not employ "hindsight bias", i.e. judging historical events and persons according to modern standards of morality. For example, George Washington and Thomas Jefferson should not be condemned as morally evil men for owning slaves in an age when slavery in one form or another (e.g. serfdom) was still common practice throughout the world.

- The course would have to look at events and individuals in the historical context.

After a couple of meetings and some negotiation about including works by Thomas Sowell and Ayaan Hirsi Ali in the list of recommended readings, the course was approved for a one-year trial period by a vote of 4 to 3. The course was recognized as an Advanced Placement ("AP) course, and the curriculum also won praise from the Alliance for Constructive Ethnic Studies. The school board subsequently unanimously approved the curriculum as a permanent course after the one-year trial period.

The most controversial measure for the Paso Robles Joint Unified School District was our resolution banning Critical Race Theory adopted in August 2021 after a total of three board meetings with some lively discussion. Many speakers argued during public comment that CRT was not even being taught in our schools and that a ban on CRT would be tantamount to whitewashing history. There were, of course, no courses on CRT, and we did not have much, if any, CRT-based content in our schools. However, we were aware of the reports about CRT training in other schools throughout the country and especially in California. CRT had also been discussed a few months earlier in connection with the ethnic studies course. A fellow board member

Dorian Baker suggested to me that we take preemptive action in our district, and I immediately agreed to draft a corresponding resolution.

I wanted to make sure when drafting the resolution, a copy of which is attached as **Appendix II**, that we provided clear and enforceable guidance for our staff. A resolution stating in general, "We hereby ban Critical Race Theory" would have been completely useless because the term "Critical Race Theory" is meaningless as a stand-alone term in a document intended to be a directive for staff, and the term too vague to be enforceable. Our Paso Robles resolution has been used as a model, for example, in the Temecula Valley Unified School District in Southern California, where the new conservative majority on the school board adopted a resolution condemning racism that was almost a duplicate of our Paso Robles resolution and a resolution banning the teaching of Critical Race Theory that was modeled to a great extent on the Paso Robles ban.[6]

A brief tour through the Paso Robles resolution will help you understand how to take similar action in other school districts and perhaps elsewhere. The first eight "whereas" clauses define terms and state, in general, the reasons for the ban on CRT, but these clauses do not contain any operative language to actually ban anything. The last three "whereas" clauses refer to the school board's legal authority to determine the curriculum within the parameters set by law and require teachers to teach the approved curriculum. Contrary to what many people believe, it is settled law that teachers in grades K-12 do not have academic freedom and freedom of speech when "on the clock" in class (comprehensively explained in a letter on First Amendment rights of staff and students circulated in the school district in August 2021, copy attached as **Appendix III**).

The general clause at the start of the operative language first states the basic policy that the school district rejects Critical Race Theory. The subsequent numbered clauses address five specific foundational elements of CRT, namely, the redefinition of racism as "racial prejudice + power", the basic assumption that racism is ordinary, the usual way society does business, interest convergence, differential racialization, and the voice of color thesis. The resolution does not address "race as a social construct" because that concept is generally valid, and the resolution also makes no mention of "intersectionality" because that concept is basically nothing more than a statement of the obvious fact that an individual can be classified in various ways.

The lettered items then list specific doctrines derived from Critical Race Theory that cannot be taught. This list includes points that have also been listed in state statutes banning the teaching of CRT in grades K-12. With regard to each lettered item, the question was whether we should allow our children to be taught these statements as gospel. For example, how can anyone support teaching students that they are inherently racist or sexist due to their race or sex (point a)? Nobody in their right mind could possibly support teaching students that someone is inherently morally or otherwise superior to others because of race or sex (point c). Who could possibly support teaching children generational and collective guilt based on race or sex (point e) or that someone should feel psychological distress on account of that person's race or sex (point f). No sane person can possibly argue that meritocracy, a hard work ethic, or the scientific method are racist or were created as tools of oppression (point g – What does this say about the people who drafted the NMAAHC "Whiteness Chart"). Point h dismisses the 1619 Project.

The final operational clause follows the lettered items and permits instruction about Critical Race Theory and its flaws as a means of "vaccinating" our students against the CRT virus, which they will certainly encounter at college. This clause may have gone a bit too far for many teachers because no social studies course has yet taught about CRT, perhaps because no instructor is yet informed what Critical Race Theory actually is.

Adopting a resolution banning Critical Race Theory requires, of course, that the item is first put on the school board's agenda. That was not a problem in Paso Robles because the subject was raised by board members. What to do if school board members refuse to address the issue of Critical Race Theory, especially after irate parents have found CRT-based propaganda in teaching materials? In California, section 35145.5 of the Education Code states with regard to school districts with grades K-12:

> It is the intent of the Legislature that members of the public be able to place matters directly related to school district business on the agenda of school district governing board meetings.

There is an equivalent provision for junior college districts in section 72121.5 Cal. Ed Code. A member of the public accordingly has the right to demand that an item "directly related to school district business" be put on the agenda. The use of CRT propaganda in school instruction is an issue directly related to school district business, so a member of the public can require that the issue be put on the agenda.

The school district cannot unreasonably delay putting the item on the agenda and should address the item within e.g. 30 days in order to avoid a risk of litigation.[7] The form in which an item is put on the agenda (action item or information item) is at the discretion of the board and the people who set the agenda. There is no guarantee that the school board will actually take any action. I recall one instance involving a request from a member of the public for an item completely unrelated to CRT to be put on the agenda. I put the matter on as an information item. When the board came to that agenda item during the meeting, I first asked for public comment; there was none. I then asked the board members if any of them wanted to say anything about the item. Nobody wanted to say anything, and the meeting moved on after spending perhaps 30 seconds on the item. Of course, a board could just as easily skip past an agenda item about CRT put on the agenda at the request of a member of the public, but not before taking public comment on the item.

The type of resolution adopted in Paso Robles effectively prevents teachers from indoctrinating students in grades K-12 with CRT propaganda. But what about colleges and universities where freedom of speech and academic freedom are much more widely acknowledged than in grades K-12? Whether or not such a ban and any disciplinary measures against instructors would be upheld in the courts is an issue that would involve substantial and lengthy litigation, and whether or not a ban would survive a challenge in the courts is an open question.

One possibility for faster, more direct impact involves funding. Critical Race Theory has been able to spread throughout academia because there has been generous funding for hiring professors who teach CRT and spread it further through academia. DEI training in universities and colleges is also funded to a great extent by the taxpayer.

State legislatures and departments of education should follow Florida's lead and reconsider whether they want to spend so much money on the divisive, racist ideology of Critical Race Theory. Indeed, probably the most effective way to counter CRT in institutions of higher learning is to "starve the beast". However, legislative action at the state level will only happen when the electorate recognizes the divisive, racist nature of CRT and politicians raise CRT as an election issue.

Chapter Summary

There has been little opposition to the spread of Critical Race Theory until the last few years. CRT found fertile ground in American institutions of higher learning where collectivist ideologies and their purveyors, for example, Marxism and Herbert Marcuse, have been enthusiastically welcomed for decades and where opposition was subdued, to put it mildly, due to fears of being called, "Racist!" Now the ideological debate is in full force, and, with your knowledge about the theory and practice of CRT, you should feel free to engage. Of course, the debate should be conducted by both sides with civil discourse.

Watch for CRT indoctrination seeping into your local cities and schools. The book *Our Skin* is just one example of how insidious such indoctrination can be, especially when directed toward small children. Make use of public comment and other opportunities to raise the issue of CRT before local school boards, junior college district boards, and city councils. When appropriate, especially in states where there are no state statutes banning the teaching of CRT in grades K-12, urge local school boards to adopt resolutions similar to what Paso Robles Joint Unified School District adopted. Finally, challenge candidates for public office at all levels to state their positions on Critical Race Theory.

---

[1]   David R. Roediger, "The Historic Foundations of Race", NMAAHC, https://nmaahc.si.edu/learn/talking-about-race/topics/historical-foundations-race.

[2]   "race (n.2)" at https://www.etymonline.com/word/race (accessed on April 16, 2023).

[3]   Alistair Bonnett, "Asia Has Its Own Strands of Racism. It's Time to Take Them Seriously", The Diplomat (June 9, 2022) at

https://thediplomat.com/2022/06/asia-has-its-own-strands-of-racism-its-time-to-take-them-seriously/.

⁴   Dylan Abad, The Associated Press, "5 Florida children charged in race attacks on white students", at News Channel 8 (March 11, 2022), https://www.wfla.com/news/florida/5-florida-children-charged-in-race-attacks-on-white-students/ .

⁵   Stanley Kurtz, "DeSantis Exposes College Board's Apparent Deceptions on AP African-American Studies", National Review (February 9, 2023), https://www.nationalreview.com/corner/desantis-exposes-college-boards-apparent-deceptions-on-ap-african-american-studies/ .

⁶   Allyson Vergara, "Critical Race Theory banned by Temecula school board", The Press Enterprise (December 13, 2022, updated 14 December 14, 2022), https://www.pressenterprise.com/2022/12/13/critical-race-theory-debated-by-temecula-school-board/ .

⁷   "Requests for the Public to Place Items on Board Agenda (K-12)", School & College Legal Services of California (February 4, 2016), available at https://sclscal.org/requests-for-the-public-to-place-items-on-board-agenda-k-12/#_ftn1.

Final Words

The ideological conflict of our age in American society and in much of the Western world is between the concept of equal protection under the law for all individuals and the collectivist, racist doctrines embodied in Critical Race Theory. CRT has already led to lowering standards and dumbing down the American people. CRT and its progenitor Marxism and their foundational, simple-minded dialectic of "oppressor" versus "oppressed" are completely unsuited as a basis for understanding a complex, technological society such as the United States consisting of over 330 million individuals with high levels of geographic and social mobility. While Marxism views "class" (bourgeoisie and proletariat) as the fault line along which society will collapse, Critical Race Theory divides society along the line of race. Marxism failed to take root in the West due to the demonstrable superiority of decentralized capitalism over centrally controlled economies and resulting social mobility. Membership in the "oppressed" and the "oppressor" economic classes in society is fluid, so that economic class is not the fault line along which American society could break.

The situation could well change as Critical Race Theory spreads. Membership in the social construct of a race in America is generally determined on the basis of physical appearance, namely, skin color and other external features. Those features, unlike economic class, are not fluid and cannot be changed (barring the miracles of medical science). Therefore, the fault line for breaking American society is much more static and deep under CRT.

The extensive and cumbersome academic writings on Critical Race Theory and the way it is played down in much of the media cannot diminish the fact that CRT is much more than an intellectual pursuit. Critical Race Theory is also a racist, social, and political movement to fundamentally change, indeed break American society by replacing the primacy of individual citizens holding individual rights with the primacy of collectivist racial identities that override individual merit and individual responsibility.

The American people as a whole and every individual American must make a fundamental decision:

> Do we want to live in a country in which racial identity is of no importance for how we live together in a pluralist, heterogeneous society where people are judged "by the content of their character and not the color of their skin?"

OR

> Do we want to live in a nation with permanent racial division and hostility in which our individual ethnic origins dictate our personal lives?

In June 2023

Postscript

The U.S. Supreme Court issued its decision prohibiting the consideration of race in college admissions on June 30, 2023, just after the editing of this book was virtually finished.[1] This landmark decision (*"SFFA v. Harvard/UNC"*) has now unambiguously established the fundamental concept under the Equal Protection Clause in the 14th Amendment: "Eliminating racial discrimination means eliminating all of it."[2] The Supreme Court has clearly answered the question posed at the end of the chapter Final Words: Americans will live in a society in which people are judged by the content of their character and not the color of their skin.

Although *SFFA v. Harvard/UNC* does not expressly mention Critical Race Theory, the decision and especially the dissenting opinions discuss and, in part, rely on fundamental aspects of CRT. The Court's opinion, delivered by Chief Justice Roberts, emphasizes the importance of the individual and rejects differentiating between individual students as members of different racial groups: "[T]he student must be treated based on his or her experiences as an individual – not on the basis of race."[3] The Court's Opinion continues:

> Many universities have for too long done just the opposite. And in doing so, they have concluded, wrongly, that the touchstone of an individual's identity is not challenges bested, skills built, or lessons learned but the color of their skin. Our constitutional history does not tolerate that choice.[4]

Justice Thomas, in his concurring opinion, expressly acknowledges the only accurate premise in CRT, according to which race is a social construct. However, he points out that racial categories can shift as views in society shift and that race cannot serve as a basis for differentiating between individuals in the law:

[R]ace is a social construct; we may each identify as members of particular races for any number of reasons, having to do with our skin color, our heritage, or our cultural identity. And, over time, these ephemeral, socially constructed categories have often shifted. For example, whereas universities today would group all white applicants together, white elites previously sought to exclude Jews and other white immigrant groups from higher education. In fact, it is impossible to look at an individual and know definitively his or her race; some who would consider themselves black, for example, may be quite fair skinned. Yet, university admissions policies ask individuals to identify themselves as belonging to one of only a few reductionist racial groups. With boxes for only "black," "white," "Hispanic," "Asian," or the ambiguous "other," how is a Middle Eastern person to choose? Someone from the Philippines? ... Whichever choice he makes (in the event he chooses to report a race at all), the form silos him into an artificial category. Worse, it sends a clear signal that the category matters.

But, under our Constitution, race is irrelevant, as the Court acknowledges. In fact, all racial categories are little more than stereotypes, suggesting that immutable characteristics somehow conclusively determine a person's ideology, beliefs, and abilities. Of course, that is false.[5]

Justice Thomas also recognizes that consideration of race in college admissions imposes, in effect, generational guilt on individuals who have nothing to do with past oppression.

Today's 17-yearolds, after all, did not live through the Jim Crow era, enact or enforce segregation laws, or take any action to oppress or enslave the victims of the past. Whatever their skin color, today's youth simply are not responsible for instituting the segregation of the 20th century, and they do not shoulder the moral debts of their ancestors. Our Nation should not punish today's youth for the sins of the past.[6]

Justice Sotomayor, in her dissenting opinion, uses the fundamental premise in CRT that American society is generally racist, even today.

[The majority opinion] is also grounded in the illusion that racial inequality was a problem of a different generation. Entrenched racial inequality remains a reality today. That is true for society writ large and, more specifically, for Harvard and the University of North Carolina (UNC), two institutions with a long history of racial exclusion. Ignoring race will not equalize a society that is racially unequal. What was true in the 1860s, and again in 1954, is true today: Equality requires acknowledgment of inequality.[7]

The "racial inequality" to which she refers has nothing to do with racial discrimination in the law. Neither she nor Justice Jackson, in her dissenting opinion, argues that the law still treats people differently based on race. Instead, both Justice Sotomayor and Justice Jackson refer to socio-economic disparities between ethnic groups.[8] Critical Race Theory's fundamental premise, according to which racism is how American society generally functions today, takes the same approach (see, Chapter IV section 1). Justice Sotomayor, with whom Justices Jackson and Kagan agree, clearly accepts CRT's fundamental premise when she describes American society as "an endemically segregated society where race has always mattered and continues to

THE CRITICAL RACE THEORY $CAM

matter,"[9] and when Justice Sotomayor argues that "[s]ystemic inequities disadvantaging underrepresented racial minorities exist beyond school resources."[10]

SFFA v. Harvard/UNC will have far-reaching effects beyond eliminating race as a criterion for admission to colleges and universities. Justice Gorsuch points out in his concurring opinion that the analysis applied by the Supreme Court in *SFFA v. Harvard/UNC* also applies far beyond academia, specifically Title VI, which prohibits recipients of federal funds from discriminating on the basis of race, and Title VII, which prohibits racial discrimination by employers.[11] This will clearly have an impact on DEI policies in federal, state and local government agencies as well as businesses. Companies that engage in "reverse discrimination" under DEI programs, no matter how subtle the racial preferences, may well find themselves facing law suits alleging racial discrimination against Whites and Asians. The proponents of CRT will find it virtually impossible, in the long run, to implement race-based measures such as reparations that give preferential treatment to members of a specific ethnic group at the expense of individuals in other ethnic groups.

However, *SFFA v. Harvard/UNC* does not mean that Critical Race Theory is suddenly a moot topic in American society. CRT-based policies are directed towards creating "equity". i.e. equality of outcome. The two main approaches for accomplishing this are (i) granting preferential treatment to members of a race with "affirmative action" and (ii) lowering or eliminating standards. The decision in *SFFA v. Harvard/UNC* will likely stop preferential treatment on the basis of race, albeit probably only after a few more a few more cases involving preferential treatment in different contexts have been litigated.

SFFA v. Harvard/UNC does not, however, affect the second approach for achieving "equity" by lowering or eliminating standards. For example, universities are still free to ignore standardized test scores in the admissions process. Therefore, the proponents of CRT can be expected to switch their focus from obtaining preferential treatment for individuals based on race to fighting "systemic racism" by redoubling their efforts to eliminate and lower standards. This could, in turn, accelerate a "race to the bottom" for America. The intellectual and political debate about Critical Race Theory is far from over.

In July 2023

---

1   *Students for Fair Admissions, Inc. v. President and Fellows of Harvard College*, 800 U.S. ____ (2023), case No. 20-1199, combined with the case No. 21-707 involving the University of North Carolina; text of majority opinion, concurring opinions and dissenting opinions available at https://www.supremecourt.gov/opinions/22pdf/20-1199_hgdj.pdf. This pdf data file has 237 pages. Each component (Syllabus, Opinion of the Court, Thomas concurring opinion. Gorsuch concurring opinion, Thomas concurring opinion, Kavanaugh concurring opinion, Sotomayor dissenting opinion, Jackson dissenting opinion) has separately numbered pages. The footnotes below refer to the numbered page in the specific component

2   Opinion of the Court, pg. 15.

3   Opinion of the Court, pg. 40.

4   Ibid.

5   Thomas concurring, pp. 47, 48.

6   Thomas concurring, pg. 45.

7   Sotomayor dissenting, pg. 17.

8   Sotomayor dissenting, pg. 21; Jackson dissenting, pp. 11 et seq.

9   Sotomayor dissenting, pg. 2.

[10]   Sotomayor dissenting, pg. 19.
[11]   Gorsuch concurring, pp. 4 et seq.

NOTE ON APPENDICES:

Appendix I, Appendix II and Appendix III are public documents of the Paso Robles Joint Unified School District. The text in the Appendices has been reformatted for this book. The Appendices are not subject to copyright and can accordingly be used as a model for similar efforts in other school districts.

Appendix I
PRJUSD Resolution Condemning Racism

PASO ROBLES JOINT UNIFIED SCHOOL DISTRICT

Resolution Condemning Racism
Resolution 21-20

"I have a dream that my four little children will one day live in a nation where they will not be judged by the color of their skin but by the content of their character."
(Dr. Martin Luther King, 1963)

WHEREAS racism has no place in American society and especially not in the Paso Robles Joint Unified School District ("PRJUSD" or the "District");

WHEREAS every person has a constitutional right to equal protection under the law; and

WHEREAS every person involved in the PRJUSD, regardless whether a student, a parent, an employee, an administrator or a volunteer, shares responsibility for promoting and maintaining a nurturing, safe, academic environment in which every student has the opportunity to make the most of the education offered by the PRJUSD; and

WHEREAS racist conduct is hurtful to individuals against whom such conduct is directed as well as harmful to a nurturing, safe, academic environment; and

223

WEREAS the PRJUSD has a Board Policy ("BP") on non-discrimination in the District's programs and activities (BP 0410) and Administrative Regulations ("AR") which impose sanctions on any student or employee who engages in racist conduct (AR 5131.2, AR 5145.3, AR 5195.9, AR 5144.1); and

WHEREAS there have been incidents of racist conduct within the purview of the PRJUSD in recent years in violation of existing policy and regulations;

NOW, THEREFORE, be it resolved by the Board of Trustees of the Paso Robles Joint Unified School District:

1. The Board of Trustees will not tolerate racism and racist conduct in any form and will take all measures to prevent and punish racism and racist conduct;

2. The Board of Trustees directs the District administration to review all Board Policies and Administrative Regulations for the purpose of strengthening the ability of the District to train staff, enforce and to impose sanctions on individuals who engage in racist conduct, including especially the use of racial slurs; and

3. The Board of Trustees directs all employees and volunteers to report instances of racist conduct to school site administrators (i.e., principals); and the PRJUSD urges all students, parents, and any other person to also report instances of racist conduct to site administrators or the District's superintendent.

ADOPTED this twenty-third day of March, 2021,

RESOLUTION 21-27A
RESOLUTION OF THE BOARD OF TRUSTEES OF THE PASO ROBLES JOINT UNIFIED SCHOOL DISTRICT
PROHIBITING THE TEACHING OF CRITICAL RACE THEORY

WHEREAS, racism has no place in American society and especially not in the Paso Robles Joint Unified School District ("PRJUSD" or the "District");

WHEREAS, the PRJUSD condemns racism and will not tolerate racism and racist conduct (see, Board Resolution 21-20 dated March 23, 2021;

WHEREAS, Critical Race Theory ("CRT") is an ideology based on false assumptions about the United States of America and its population;

WHEREAS, the definitional foundation of Critical Race Theory involving an artificial distortion of the traditional definition of "racism" is fatally flawed;

WHEREAS, Critical Race Theory is a divisive ideology that assigns moral fault to individuals solely on the basis of an individual's race and, therefore, is itself a racist ideology;

WHEREAS, Critical Race Theory assigns generational guilt and racial guilt for conduct and policies that are long in the past;

WHEREAS, Critical Race Theory violates the fundamental principle of equal protection under the law;

WHEREAS, Critical Race Theory views social problems primarily as racial problems and, thus, detracts from analysis of underlying socio-economic causes of social problems;

WHEREAS, the Board of Trustees of the PRJUSD has the legal authority to determine the curriculum taught in the PRJUSD within the parameters set by law;

WHEREAS, the Board of Trustees can require teachers to teach the curriculum approved by the Board of Trustees;

WHEREAS, the laws of the United States of America and the State of California do not require that Critical Race Theory be taught in public schools (grades K-12);

NOW, THEREFORE, BE IT RESOLVED on the 10th day of August, 2021, by the Board of Trustees of the Paso Robles Joint Unified School District:

Critical Race Theory is rejected and will not constitute the basis for any instruction in the PRJUSD. The following specific elements of Critical Race Theory cannot be taught:

1. Racism is racial prejudice plus power, a concept that is often used to argue that (i) only individuals classified as "white" people can be racist because only "white" people control society and (ii) individuals in ethnic minorities cannot be racist because they do not control society.

2. Racism is ordinary, the usual way society does business.

3. "Interest convergence" or "material determinism", according to which the incentive to move away from racist policies depends primarily on the self-interest of the oppressor class, i.e. "whites".

4. "Differential racialization", according to which the "dominant society racializes different minority groups at different times, in response to different needs such as the labor market";[1]

---

[1] Richard Delgado and Jean Stefancic, Critical Race Theory, An Introduction, 3rd ed. (2017), p. 10.

5. The "voice-of-color" thesis, according to which merely "minority status ... brings with it a presumed competence to speak about race and racism",[2] a concept often used to discredit opposing arguments on the basis of the opposing person's race;

FURTHERMORE, the following doctrines derived from Critical Race Theory cannot be taught:

a. An individual, by virtue of his or her race or sex, is inherently racist and/or sexist, whether consciously or unconsciously.

b. Individuals are either a member of the oppressor class or the oppressed class because of race or sex.

c. An individual is inherently morally or otherwise superior to another individual because of race or sex.

d. An individual should be discriminated against or receive adverse treatment due to the individual's race or sex, or an individual should receive favorable treatment due to the individual's race or sex.

e. An individual, by virtue of his or her race or sex, bears responsibility for actions committed in the past or present by other members of the same race or sex.

f. An individual should feel discomfort, guilt, anguish or any other form of psychological distress on account of his or her race or sex.

g. Meritocracy or traits such as, but not limited to, a hard work ethic or the scientific method are racist or sexist or were created by members of a particular race to oppress members of another race.

h. The advent of slavery in the territory that is now the United States constituted the true founding of the United

---

[2] I(bid., p. 11

States, or the preservation of slavery was a material motive for independence from England.

Notwithstanding the above restrictions, social science courses can include instruction about Critical Race Theory, provided that such instruction plays only a subordinate role in the overall course and provided further that such instruction focuses on the flaws in Critical Race Theory.

ADOPTED this 10th day of August 2021, on motion of Trustee Baker, seconded by Trustee Gannon, on the following roll call vote:

August 18, 2021

Dear Teachers, Staff, Students, Parents and the Community,

As many of you may recall, a year ago as we opened school in solely distance learning, some issues arose that begged the question of what materials can be displayed in the video backgrounds of our students while participating in remote learning. This also led to a discussion about the question of what teachers can display in their video backgrounds, e.g. on the walls of their virtual and/or real classrooms. These two questions involved an analysis of the First Amendment rights of students while participating at school (whether in person or via distance learning), as well as the rights of our public employees while working. There are well-established laws and long-established District policies governing such matters, some of which we have summarized below to assist in educating staff and students regarding such matters. In the last year, the Supreme Court has also clarified some guidance on the school role in social media.

Additionally, the subject of a specific controversial issue, Critical Race Theory, has become very heated around the nation. The Board of Trustees has passed Resolution 21-27A (attached) to provide additional specific guidance to the direction to staff so that no one unintentionally or otherwise violates the Board's direction on this matter.

1. **Students**

   Students do not surrender their right to free speech when they attend school. This has been clear since the landmark decision 52 years ago by the U.S. Supreme Court in Tinker v. Des Moines Independent Community

School District, 393 U.S. 503 (1969). That case held that free speech can only be limited if the school can prove that the speech in question "materially and substantially interferes" with school operations, in other words, that the speech is "disruptive". The permitted speech also should not violate the rights of other protected classes.

The U.S. Supreme Court provided further guidance on what constitutes "disruptive" speech in the case of Bethel School Dist. No. 403 v. Fraser, 478 U.S. 675 (1986). The Court also set forth some limitations on the rights of free speech of students in Morse v. Frederick, 127 S. Ct. 2618 (2007). In Morse, the school prohibited a student from displaying a flag that the District believed promoted illegal drug use. The Court stated that the "First Amendment does not require schools to tolerate at school events student expression that contributes to those dangers." More recently, in Mahanoy Area School District v B.L. (2021), in an 8-1 decision, the Supreme Court ruled that the Mahanoy Area School District's decision to suspend a student from the cheerleading team for posting vulgar language and gestures on social media (outside of school hours and away from the school's campus) violated the First Amendment. Importantly, this ruling did not compromise the Tinker Decision. The Court clearly found the penalty of a year's suspension from cheerleading to be excessive, and didn't see how the post "negatively and substantially disrupted school" and did not violate the rights of a protected class.

Moreover, Education Code section 48950 allows districts to regulate student speech that is libelous, slanderous, or obscene, or which incites students to create a clear and present danger of substantial interruption of the orderly operation of school. Consistent with this legal scheme, District policies prohibit students' speech which promotes illegal activities or violence and speech, which is profane, which violates the rights of a protected class and/or substantially is disruptive to the orderly operation of school.

The fact that a teacher or other students disagree with the speech does NOT mean that the speech is "disruptive". The school district has a fundamental duty to protect the proper exercise of free speech under the First Amendment and cannot permit a "heckler's veto". If anyone has an issue with what a student says in the proper exercise of free speech, the proper response is to engage in civil discourse and also exercise one's own right of free speech.

For clarification, some practical examples have been analyzed below to illustrate what is permitted, on the one hand, and what is prohibited, on the other hand, with respect to in students' video backgrounds. (Bear in mind that these examples are subject to the condition that otherwise permitted content might still cross the line into being "disruptive" depending on the specific circumstances of a case).

- Signs, banners etc. supporting a political candidate / party / state proposition / or cause (e.g. BLM, thin blueline, CRT, etc.)	Permitted
- Flags	Permitted
- Religious symbols	Permitted
- Gang symbols, the swastika and other emblems of groups dedicated to crime	Not permitted.

- Representations and containers of alcoholic beverages / drugs and paraphernalia / overly sexual suggestive material	Not permitted
- Profanity (also if part of otherwise permitted materials)	Not permitted

This list is by no means exhaustive or conclusive, especially when we consider the creativity of our young people. The general concept, however, is that displayed material cannot be "disruptive," so use common sense.

2. Teachers

The general rule when teachers are off the job is that they have the same right to free speech as anyone else. However, the purpose of this section is to discuss the limits on teachers' rights to free speech when they are "on the clock".

The U.S. Supreme Court held in the case of Garcetti v. Ceballos, 547 U.C. 410 (2006) that public employees are not insulated from employer discipline under the First Amendment when they make statements pursuant to their official duties. Teachers speak on behalf of the school district when performing their duties and accordingly must comply with school policy on controversial subjects. Brown v. Chicago Board of Education, No. 15-1857 (7th Cir. 2016). Courts have consistently held that when teachers make statements, advocate for particular points of view, and/or post specific items on walls or bulletin boards – they are acting pursuant to their official duties and their speech is not protected under the First Amendment. We refer our teachers to our attached policy 6161.11, which is consistent with case law, and reads in part:

"In the classroom, teachers act on behalf of the district and are expected to follow the adopted curriculum. In leading or guiding discussions about issues that may be controversial, a teacher may not advocate his/her personal opinion or viewpoint..." (emphasis added).

Simply stated: Classroom materials are supposed to relate to the curriculum, and the teacher is supposed to take a neutral position on controversial issues. We recognize that "taking a neutral position" is not always as simple as it sounds, but our teachers are professionals who can make the right determination in virtually all cases. We now provide some practical examples of what a teacher cannot display in the classroom or in the teachers' background (the virtual classroom):

- Signs, banners etc. supporting a political candidate / party / state proposition	Not permitted, unless part of the curriculum (e.g. class on current events with such materials used as visual aids) and as possible representing multiple viewpoints and preferably positive not negative in substance

- Signs, banners etc. supporting social causes (e.g. BLM, CRT, thin blue line etc.)	Materials related to social causes of a political nature are not permitted in classes where there is no connection to the district curriculum. They are permitted and encouraged if relevance to the curriculum is readily evident. *A timely example might be a Civics class where both BLM and Blue Line Flags could be displayed with an assignment for students to write an opinion piece showing how it is possible*
- Flags	The US and California flags can always be shown because they are part of the standard furnishings in our classrooms; other flags are subject to a case by case analysis and should not be posted if to promote an idea
- Signs or banners that promote a religious viewpoint	Not permitted unless used as visual aids in curriculum

We ask our teachers to ask their principals or the District Office if they have any questions about whether an item is appropriate for display in the background during distance learning or later in the classroom.

With regard to Critical Race Theory (CRT), the Board has basically agreed with many of its supporters in ordering it not be taught in our K-12 schools. I have attached to this memorandum a copy of the resolution that was passed by the Board. It lists specific elements of CRT that are not to be introduced nor taught as part of the formal district curriculum. Staff are directed by me to comply with the directives of the Board detailed in the resolution.

If any teachers have questions about my direction in this memo, they are encouraged to ask for clarification and specific answers to specific questions. Teachers may wish to go through their department if secondary, or directly to their site principal. I am also available at any time to respond in writing, and/or to meet with any concerned staff. Please ask for clarification in advance, if possible, of any potentially problematic discussion and remember with the last year of Distance Learning and Hybrid methods of instruction, many parents have taken, and will continue to take, much more active roles in review of what is being taught in our classes. This is our new reality which we must embrace not discourage.

*****

We welcome and appreciate the diversity of ideas of both our teachers and our students. We have provided this letter and analysis in order to facilitate an understanding of the rights of each and how to protect those rights. The District is committed to protecting the free speech rights of our students and complies with our responsibilities concerning controversial issues. The role of the District and our staff and educators is not to convince our students one way or another on controversial issues. Instead, our purpose is to teach our students how to analyze and debate controversial issues in civil discourse. We greatly appreciate your support and understanding during these unprecedented times. I am proud to work in such a supportive educational community, and thank you in advance for your adherence to District policy and legal requirements as we navigate these issues together for the collective good of our students.

Please contact me with any questions or concerns.

Curt Dubost, Superintendent

Index

Printed in the USA
CPSIA information can be obtained
at www.ICGtesting.com
LVHW021651091123
763115LV00101B/1313/J